SCANDINAVIA
DENMARK, FINLAND, ICELAND, NORWAY AND SWEDEN

Welcome to Scandinavia

Sylvie Nickels

Collins
Glasgow and London

Cover Photographs
J. Allan Cash Ltd: Arctic Circle (top), Geirangerfjord (mid l.),
Koli (mid rt), Esbjerg (btm)

Photographs
J. Allan Cash Ltd.
pp. 40 (l.), 47 (inset), 58 (inset), 61, 62, 64, 69, 72 (bkgrd and inset: top l.), 88 (l.),
90, 94, 95, 96, 102 (l., rt), 104, 107, 113 (inset), 116 (btm), 121 (top), 123

Danish Tourist Board
pp. 35 (btm), 36, 48, 49, 50, 51, 52

Solarfilma, Iceland
p. 72 (inset: rt)

Van Phillips
pp. 35 (top), 39, 40 (rt), 41, 46–7 (bkgrd), 82 (inset: top l., rt), 97

Photobank
pp. 77, 78, 86 (rt), 88 (rt), 103, 116 (top), 117 (top)

Picturepoint Ltd.
pp. 58 (bkgrd), 59, 60, 67, 72 (inset: btm l.), 76, 82 (bkgrd and inset: btm l.), 86 (l.),
87, 105, 106, 113 (bkgrd), 120, 121 (btm), 122

Swedish Tourist Board
pp. 109, 117 (btm)

Town Plans
M. and R. Piggott

Illustration
pp. 6–7 Peter Joyce

Regional Maps
Mike Shand, Iain Gerard

First published 1983
Copyright © text: Sylvie Nickels 1983
Copyright © maps: Wm. Collins, Sons & Co. Ltd.
Published by William Collins Sons and Company Limited
Printed in Great Britain

ISBN 0 00 447324 8

HOW TO USE THIS BOOK

The contents page of this book shows how the countries are divided up into tourist
regions. The book is in two main sections: general information and gazetteer. The
latter is arranged in the tourist regions with an introduction and a regional map
(detail below left). There are also plans of main cities (detail below right). All
main entries listed in the gazetteer are shown on the regional maps. Places
to visit and leisure facilities available in each region and city are indicated
by symbols. Main roads, railways and airports are shown on the maps.

Regional Maps

- 🖼 Museum/gallery
- ✝ Religious building
- ✈ Main airport
- ✈ Other airport
- 🏰 Castle/fortress
- ▲ Climbing/mountainous
- ⊞ Interesting building
- ⛵ Boating/sailing
- ❊ Gardens
- 🎡 Amusement park
- ⛷ Skiing/winter sports

- 🐘 Zoo
- m Ancient monument
- 🌳 Park
- 🐦 Bird life
- ⛏ Mines/caves
- 🚶 Walking/hiking
- 🚣 Water sports
- 🛶 Canoeing

Town Plans

- 🖼 Museum/gallery
- ✝ Religious building
- 🏰 Castle/fortress
- ⊞ Interesting building
- 🎭 Theatre
- 📖 Library
- 🏛 Town hall
- ✉ Post office
- ℹ Information
- POL Police
- ● Park
- ❊ Garden
- ⬤ Railway station
- 🚌 Bus terminal
- Ⓟ Car park

metres	feet
1500	4921
1000	3281
500	1640
200	656
0	0

————	motorway
= = = =	motorway under construction
————	other roads
———	railway

CONTENTS

Regions

SCANDINAVIA

If there is one commodity that Scandinavia has more than most holiday regions it is space: an infinity caught between mountains, forests, lakes, fjords or rolling sand dunes. The statistics speak for themselves. The combined areas of Denmark, Finland, Iceland, Norway and Sweden (nearly 1,300,000sq km/500,000sq mi) would swallow up the UK comfortably five times over or cover most of Alaska; yet the total population of around 20 million is less than those of London and New York put together. And to go with all that space are the amenities which the sun-worshipping Nordic nations make the best possible use of during their short but often brilliant summers.

From the south of Denmark at latitude 55°N to Norway's North Cape at latitude 71°N, this enormous area embraces a great variety of terrain and climate. Much of Denmark, moulded by good husbandry, has the homely quality of the English countryside, and weather patterns are similar too. Western Norway's dramatic, tortuous fjords bite deep into the mountainous spine that forms much of the border with neighbouring Sweden. From it, the rivers pour down through the Swedish valleys that range from the grandiose to the gently mellow to reach the Gulf of Bothnia and the Baltic Sea via tens of thousands of lakes and a vast acreage of forest or farmland. Finland is more of the same, relatively low lying so that its huge horizons seem to add an extra dimension, interrupted by parallel ridges left by the last Ice Age. The north of Scandinavia is rather loosely referred to as Lapland – that area of northern Norway, Sweden and Finland where a few tens of thousands of the Lapps, or Same people, live in lonely landscapes characterized by bare-topped fells, sparse forests and rolling tundra north of the Arctic Circle. It is a region where the sun shines 24 hours a day for up to six weeks around midsummer, depending on latitude, matched by a similar period around midwinter when it does not shine at all. Yet winter nights rarely have the velvet darkness of more 'southern latitudes, for the sky flares for hours with colour from the invisible sun, the snow adds an eerie luminosity, and on the coldest clearest nights the aurora borealis (northern lights) sends magic veils rippling silently above the land. Finally, far out to sea, Iceland sits astride the Mid-Atlantic Ridge, that massive fault in the earth's crust which created volcanic landscapes that contrast with the vivid green of coastal valleys.

Administratively, each country is divided into counties or provinces, subdivided into communes (local districts or municipalities). Scandinavia's brand of democracy has resulted in a proliferation of political parties that makes for rather frequent changes of government (*eg* Finland has 12 parties, Denmark 10), often necessitating coalitions, but the trend has long been a liberal form of social democracy with a few experimental interruptions such as the present Conservative majority in Norway. The Scandinavian passion for freedom is matched by a deep sense of justice. It is significant that the post of Ombudsman, who investigates complaints against the actions of government departments, originated here (as early as 1809 in Sweden). There is also a refreshing absence of class divisions even though an impressive range of noble titles survives, especially in Sweden. Denmark, Norway and Sweden each has a constitutional monarchy (the Danes' is the oldest in Europe). Finland and Iceland are headed by Presidents appointed for several years. Finland's President Kekkonen was in office 25 years until his recent retirement (he has been succeeded by former prime minister, Maunu Koivisto). Iceland has the world's first freely elected woman head of state, Vigdis Finnbogadóttir. In all five countries, social welfare is of a high order – Sweden has one of the most advanced systems anywhere.

Though inter-Nordic cooperation binds the five countries closely together, the relationship of each with the rest of the world is very individual. Denmark is the only one to belong to the European Economic Community, though the others are all associated with the European Free Trade Association and have important trade links with the EEC. Denmark, Iceland and Norway are members of NATO, while Sweden and Finland are neutral, the latter insisting on an unequivocal policy of neutrality to maintain its finely balanced position between east and west. As far as religion is concerned,

the Lutheran Church is dominant in all five countries, though several Free Churches thrive in Sweden, while Finland has a substantial minority following the Orthodox faith.

Throughout Scandinavia, the standard of living is very high indeed. Increased mechanization and diversification in recent decades have modified dependence on the traditional occupations of agriculture in Denmark, fishing in Iceland, fishing, farming and forestry in Norway, the forest industries of Finland, and timber and iron ore in Sweden; but these are still very important. Other specialities have emerged. For example, forming the backbone of the Danish economy are innumerable small enterprises. Sweden has moved into advanced technology, especially machinery and electrical equipment, and its achievements in worker participation, notably in the car industry, are well known. Norway's North Sea oil riches have revolutionized economic life. Finland has made huge strides in the metal working industry since World War II. Iceland is currently harnessing and marketing some of the incalculable energy bottled up underground and in its thunderous waterways. Scandinavian know-how is a major invisible export, which extends to setting up paper mills in developing African countries or building luxury hotels by East Europe's Black Sea beaches. In manufacturing, a whole range of first-class products have emerged on to the world's markets, from Swedish cut glass and inexpensive furniture, Finnish fashions, Danish silver and porcelain to Norwegian knitwear.

A genuine interest in and flair for good design is common to all the Nordic peoples. The 'average' Dane, Finn, Icelander, Norwegian, Swede, really cares – and knows – who has designed the cut glass bowl, stainless steel cutlery, cups and saucers or the lampstand in daily use. They also prefer to embellish their walls with original paintings rather than reproductions, and are voracious readers of their own and the world's literature.

The toughness of much of Scandinavia's terrain and the rigorous climate for much of the year moulded the pioneer spirit which resulted in the remarkable adventures of early Scandinavian history, outlined in the next section. Similarly it has produced some of the world's greatest latter-day explorers such as Amundsen, Nansen, Nordenskiöld and Rasmussen. Scandinavians share a splendidly dry sense of humour and the ability to laugh at themselves. But there are many differences, too. The Danes are the extroverts of northern Europe, the most relaxed, the easiest to meet and know. The Norwegians and Finns are much more reserved, offering endless help if asked, although they themselves are rather self-sufficient. The Finns especially tend to a contemplativeness that can at times amount to the morose. The Swedes, temperamentally in the middle, are given to sensitivity over their material wealth and their neutrality. Language problems are minimal, however, as English is spoken to an extent that often puts to shame those who speak only their mother tongue.

Compared with more southerly parts of Europe, sights of historic or architectural interest, though many and varied, are not so thickly concentrated away from main cities and, except in Denmark, distances between can be considerable. This fact, allied to the beauty of the natural surroundings almost everywhere, makes the whole region particularly well suited to two types of holiday: those devoted to outdoor activities, and touring on a modest or grand scale by car or by public transport. Enjoy Yourself (p. 22) outlines the many facilities available for special interests, but to these must be added the sheer joy of magnificent scenery. You will soon notice, too, that the tendency for most Scandinavians to escape from their well-organized cities into the surrounding countryside at every opportunity is more than just the answer to an aesthetic need. It is also the need to feel part of nature, whether it is picking mushrooms in the woods, messing about in a boat, hewing wood or drawing water, or testing wits or stamina against some natural element.

For the purposes of touring and easy reference, each country has been divided according to size or topography as follows. **Denmark** falls naturally into two main sections: Jylland (Jutland), Fyn (Funen), Langeland and Aerø; Sjaelland (Sealand) – which includes Copenhagen – Møn, Falster and Lolland; with short summaries for Bornholm and the Faroes. (Greenland, though part of the Danish Realm, is so far away and sparsely populated that it is outside the scope of this guide.) **Finland** is split into the South covering most of the lake districts and archipelagoes; the North from Oulu through Lappi (Finnish Lapland) to its northernmost boundaries. **Iceland** is treated as one region (subdivided into North and South) because of the many possibilities for round trips. **Norway** has three sections: Eastern Norway, including Oslo and the eastern valleys; the Western Fjords covering Bergen and the famous fjord country; North Norway from Trondheim to the Soviet border, including Finnmark (Norwegian Lapland) and the North Cape. **Sweden** also comprises three sections: South Sweden including Gothenburg and all the southern provinces across to the island of Gotland; Central Sweden with Stockholm and the folkloric provinces of Dalarna and Värmland; North Sweden including most of the high mountains and Lapland up to the borders with Norway and Finland.

Though the freedom of your own four wheels has obvious advantages, the excellent public transport services outlined in Internal Travel (p. 14), and various organized tours or excursions out of main resorts, make it possible to see a great deal at reasonable cost. Magnificent scenery abounds and the subtle quality of changing light is matchless in more southerly latitudes. That is completely free.

THE PAST

Archaeological finds indicate that from a time following the retreat of the ice in the last glacial period, early man has moved over the more habitable parts of Scandinavia, food gathering, hunting and fishing. By about 1500 BC, during the Bronze Age, a people of Germanic origin occupied Denmark and southern parts of the Scandinavian peninsula where they developed a culture of villages, land cultivation, religious ritual and a high skill in craftsmanship. Numerous rock carvings date from this period. With the Iron Age and the northward extension of Roman boundaries, Scandinavia first enters written history. The Emperors Augustus and Nero sent fleets into northern waters and Pliny the Elder, Tacitus and the geographer Ptolemy were writing of what had been seen. We are even given a glimpse of some strange tribes, the Lapps and Finns living far to the north or east of the Germanic tribes of the Scandinavian peninsula.

At the beginning of the Viking era, Scandinavia had little political entity, consisting only of many provinces sharing a more or less common language. Though only loosely linked, the energetic people of these northern territories were soon to make their fearful and forceful mark on European history. By the middle of the 8th century, their shipwrights had developed sailing craft to a remarkable standard: high-prowed long ships, fine examples of which are preserved in the museums at Roskilde, Oslo and elsewhere. It was not as farmers or traders that the Vikings were to be first known, but as raiders and robbers. Impelled by over-population in a harsh land, and no doubt also by a spirit of adventure, they roamed far across Europe for most of the 9th and 10th centuries. They made swift pirate raids at first; later, massive assaults resulted in colonizing as well as conquering. They settled in much of western Europe, including Britain and Normandy, occupied Iceland and Greenland, and even discovered North America.

It was during this time that some sort of political order was formed out of earlier disarray, and organized states emerged with well-defined boundaries ruled by monarchs with such splendid names as Erik Bloodaxe and Harald Fairhair. Denmark, under its rulers Gorm the Old, Harald Bluetooth and Svein Forkbeard, became a powerful kingdom in the 10th century; it was Harald (950–986) who brought Christianity to Denmark, and Norway under the political control of the Danish crown. The greatest of Danish Kings was Knut (Canute), king of England as well as Denmark and Norway. But Knut's over-large North Sea empire collapsed on his death when political control was reversed and Denmark now became subject to the Norwegian king Magnus the Good, until 1046. In 1064, Svein Estridsson became king of Denmark and, following many years of war with Norway, his country settled down within what were to be her boundaries for many years (for a long time they included what is today southern Sweden).

It was in this period that the first towns were founded in Denmark, the first bishoprics created and a substantial series of fortifications were constructed, including part of the Danevirke, intended to secure Jutland's southern border against Charlemagne. The Viking Age in Sweden followed a rather different course; their efforts were directed south and east rather than west, and they travelled as traders as well as raiders. Sailing Russia's great rivers they reached both Byzantium and the Caspian Sea. The Slav name for Viking was Rus – hence the name Russia.

Christianity came more slowly to Sweden, and not without resistance and bloodshed. It was well into the 12th century before it really gained a firm hold and an archbishopric was established at Uppsala. And it was Christian crusading zeal, as well as territorial greed, that brought heathen Finland under Swedish domination. Ethnically and linguistically unrelated to the Scandinavian family, the Finns are believed to have arrived from somewhere east of the Volga at about the beginning of the Christian era. Erik IX, Sweden's patron saint, moved into Finland in 1157 and, with him, helping to lead the Christian mission, was the Englishman Bishop Henry, soon to be slaughtered for his pains. Thus Christianity's first martyr in Finland became her patron saint.

Following the Viking period, the Scandinavian countries began to concentrate on their own resources and trade; timber, iron and fish products were important exports then as they are now. So profitable became this trade that the Hanseatic League of north German cities cast covetous eyes upon it, and as a result much commercial independence was lost. Norway, dependent upon the Hanseatic monopoly of grain, lost the most, and the League became a state within a state. Timbered Hanseatic warehouses by the waterfront in Bergen are reminders of this period.

Queen Margrethe I of Denmark (1352–1412) married King Haakon of Norway and, by the Union of Kalmar (1397), succeeded in uniting all three Scandinavian countries. Norway and Denmark were to remain united until 1814, but Danish rule was much resented in Sweden which finally broke away and reestablished her independence under Gustavus Vasa (1523–60). He set about improving Sweden's economic and military strength, peppering the landscape with mighty castles in the process; he also broke with Rome and adopted Lutheranism.

Rising tension erupted in a series of wars between Denmark and Norway on the one hand, and Sweden and Finland on the other. The power of the Hanseatic League was beginning to decline and Denmark gained strength because of her control of the Sound; no ship could enter the Baltic free of her toll. Sweden, on the other hand, held a meagre ice-free outlet to the North Sea, a mere 11 miles of coastline around Gothenburg which, in spite of being defended by the great fortress of Elfsborg, was several times lost to the Danes.

In 1448, the House of Oldenburg had succeeded to the throne of Denmark; now represented (since 1972) by Queen Margrethe II, it is the oldest royal dynasty in Europe. Under one of its early kings, Christian IV (1588–1648), Denmark enjoyed a period of particular prosperity and glory. Despite his robust way of life (he had a great weakness for the fair sex), he was an energetic and competent administrator and much loved by his people. It was he who was responsible for some of Copenhagen's finest buildings, including two royal palaces. He also founded countless new towns in Denmark, Norway and south Sweden, fortified Denmark's frontiers, started trading companies, promoted exploration and improved education and agriculture.

Alas, he was too ambitious and, by bringing Denmark into the Thirty Years' War, he suffered defeat first at the hands of the Germans, and later the Swedes. For Sweden, too, had the benefit of energetic and powerful kings. She achieved her greatest gains under Gustavus II Adolphus (1594–1632) who brought Sweden into the Thirty Years' War on the side of the Protestants and spread Swedish rule to Poland, the Baltic States and parts of Prussia, making the Baltic almost a Swedish lake for a time. By about the middle of the 17th century, Sweden had also finally driven Denmark from the Scandinavian peninsula and had annexed much of Norway, including a stretch of her western coastline around Trondheim. When Carl (Charles) XII ascended the Swedish throne, he inherited a stable and solvent regime, but much of Sweden's power was lost as a result of the Great Northern War (1697–1718). At first Carl was successful against Peter the Great, but he was defeated in his disastrous march on Moscow. During his many years of absence abroad, Denmark attacked south Sweden once again but unsuccessfully. Later Carl invaded Norway, but was killed by a stray bullet, and Sweden subsequently lost much of her empire.

At the dawn of the 19th century, Napoleon was to turn much of Europe into a battlefield. Gustavus IV, then king of Sweden, bitterly opposed the conqueror, but it served him ill for, following a secret treaty with Napoleon, Czar Alexander I was free to annexe Finland which, in 1809, after more than 600 years of Swedish rule, became a Grand Duchy of Russia; subsequent Czarist oppression eventually resulted in a great Finnish national revival. Meanwhile Denmark and Norway were involved on the side of France; the fierce bombardment of Copenhagen by the British was one repercussion. In the end Sweden's contribution was recognized at the Congress of Vienna (1814–15) and, as compensation for loss of Finland, Norway was ceded to Sweden. Denmark, however, continued to control an increasingly unwilling Iceland, as well as Greenland and the Faroes. Ironically, with no heir to succeed Gustavus IV, Jean-Baptiste Bernadotte, one of Napoleon's most talented marshals, was elected Crown Prince of Sweden. The line is currently represented by the seventh ruling Bernadotte, Carl XVI Gustaf who came to the throne in 1973.

The Norwegians profoundly resented Swedish domination, though it was soon to become a fairly loose tie, and they gained complete independence in 1905. Prince Carl of Denmark was elected King Haakon VII of Norway and was succeeded on his death in 1957 by the present king, Olav V.

Scandinavia remained neutral during World War I. Following the Russian Revolution, Finland declared her independence in 1917 and, after some internal struggle, took her place among the responsible small nations of the world. Iceland, formerly a Danish possession, became a sovereign state in 1918 while retaining a personal union with the Danish king; in 1944 she became an independent republic. The Faroes, though still part of the Danish kingdom, became self-governing in 1948. Greenland established Home Rule in 1979.

At the outbreak of World War II, the countries of northern Europe announced their intention to remain neutral, but in November, 1939, the Soviet Union launched the Winter War against Finland. In the peace treaty of March, 1940, Finland had to cede considerable territory to her opponent. In April, 1940, Germany invaded and occupied Denmark and Norway, the latter after considerable resistance. The Faroes and Iceland were occupied by the British in order to forestall German invasion. In 1941, the United States took over the defence of Iceland and still have a base at Keflavík.

In June, 1941, after Germany's invasion of Russia, Finland entered the war in her wake in the hope of regaining lost territory. She was forced to sign a separate treaty with the Soviet Union in September, 1944, losing again much of her eastern territory, her northern outlet to the Barents Sea and was also faced with massive war reparations. Only Sweden had been able to maintain neutrality.

THE ARTS

Despite its small population, Scandinavia has made a brave contribution to the collective creativity of the world; this often reflected the darker and more dramatic moods of its landscapes, the elements and human struggle, though quite frequently with an injection of wry humour. In modern times, few other parts of the world have made more impact on architecture and design.

Literature Runic inscriptions, from the 9th–12th centuries, giving factual details about the personalities and events of the times are the first evidence of writing. It was towards the end of this period that the greatest Norse contribution to world literature was first committed to paper. The Sagas, which for generations had been perpetuated orally, were concerned variously with historical record, romances of chivalry and mighty family epics describing lives and feuds in the 10th and 11th centuries. Most of them come from Iceland and they make robust reading. The outstanding literary figure of those times was **Snorri Sturluson** (1179–1241) whose *Heimskringla* is a history of the kings of Norway up to 1177 and whose Prose Edda covers everything from a comprehensive survey of Norse mythology to advice to young *skálds* (poets).

Apart from a wealth of ballads and religious writings, there followed a considerable gap until the 18th and especially the early 19th century, when a new sense of national identity began to emerge, along with a growing political awareness, in the less independent countries. The 18th-century humorist and philosopher **Ludvig Holberg** (1684–1754), who was born in Norway but spent most of his life in Denmark, is considered the founder of modern Danish and Norwegian literature. The religious-philosophical works of Danish **Søren Kierkegaard** (1813–55) earned him an international reputation, but it was the subtle fairytale world of **Hans Christian Andersen** (1805–75) that first gave Denmark an everlasting place in world literature.

In Norway, **Henrik Wergeland** (1808–45) wrote prolifically and fought passionately for his country's independence, but it was **Henrik Ibsen** (1828–1906) who translated social, religious and moral problems into literary themes and became a model for playwrights the world over. His contemporary, **Bjørnstjerne Bjørnson** (1832–1910), was also profoundly concerned with justice and human rights. Across the border, **August Strindberg** (1849–1912) brought Sweden squarely into the international arena with plays and novels that ranged from bitter misogyny to religious mysticism. Even more popular within Sweden was **Selma Lagerlöf** (1858–1940) who graphically portrayed life in the province of Värmland.

In Finland, a young doctor called **Elias Lönnrot** quietly collected together the folk tales published as the *Kalevala* in 1835, an epic of homeric proportions which was to help galvanize his country-men into a new awareness of their own culture. *Kalevala*'s influence was far-reaching on literature, music and art of the 19th century. First of the great Finnish writers, though he wrote in Swedish, was **Johan Ludvig Runeberg** (1804–77), but **Aleksis Kivi** (1834–72) was the first novelist and playwright to write in the Finnish language and is regarded as the father of Finnish literature; his works have an earthy quality that seems to come straight from the forests.

Among other leading Scandinavian writers of the late 19th or 20th century are Denmark's **Karen Blixen** (writing as **Isak Dinesen**), Finland's **Väinö Linna**, Iceland's **Halldór Laxness**, Norway's **Knut Hamsun** and **Sigrid Undset**, and Sweden's **Pär Lagerkvist**.

Music The two giants of Scandinavian music are the Norwegian **Edvard Grieg** (1843–1907) and Finland's **Jean Sibelius** (1865–1957); the works of both show a strong national flavour. Also important is Denmark's **Carl Nielsen** (1865–1931), a composer of independent style and strong melody.

Folk music and ballads are kept alive throughout the area, and a number of major festivals are devoted to them, as well as many local events. The tradition is particularly strong in the fjords and val-leys of Norway – the distinctive *Harding-fele* (violin with two sets of strings) for which there is no written music, origi-nated there.

Art The art of the area began with primitive rock carvings from the Stone Age (notably in north Norway) and Bronze Age (especially in south Sweden). The Vikings produced richly carved ships, sledges and artefacts, their en-twined plants and animals eventually merging with the motifs of Christianity, for example, in elaborate church carvings (notably the Norwegian stave churches, see also Architecture). Medieval churches show examples of wall paintings and fres-coes. Later came the delightful folk art decorating walls and furniture, such as the *rosemaling* (rose painting) which orig-inated in Telemark, Norway (p. 73) and the charming, god-fearing peasant art of Dalarna, Sweden (p. 109), with its biblical scenes. Dalarna also produced two im-portant painters, **Carl Larsson** (1833–1919) and **Anders Zorn** (1860–1920),

and to the same period belong the more sophisticated works of **Prince Eugen** (1865–1947).

Sometimes described as the father of Danish painting, **Christoffer Wilhelm Eckersberg** (1783–1853) pioneered the naturalism that dominated art in the 19th century. His work was roughly contem-porary with the serene classicism of the sculptor **Bertel Thorvaldsen** (1770–1844). There were many good, if not internationally known, painters in the 19th century, but when it comes to the international scene, it was Norway that produced one of the first great expression-ist painters, **Edvard Munch** (1863–1944, p. 83). In Finland, the *Kalevala* (see Literature) was making a profound impact on art, and notable painters from that period are **Albert Edelfelt** (1854–1905) and **Akseli Gallen-Kallela** (1865–1931).

Scandinavian sculptors have proved particularly successful. The works of **Gustav Vigeland** (1869–1943), which occupy an entire park in Oslo (p. 83), are moving and disturbing. Those of **Carl Milles** (1875–1955) are more exuberant and fill his own beautiful terraced gardens in a suburb of Stockholm (p. 113). A controversial painter and sculptor is Denmark's **J.F. Willumsen** (1863–1958), to whom a museum is devoted in Frederikssund. The works of Finland's **Wäinö Aaltonen** pepper his homeland, while more recently there are fine works by **Aimo Tukiainen** and **Eila Hiltunen**.

The works of both **Jóhannes Kjarval** (1885–1972) and **Ásgrímur Jónsson** (d. 1958), who was much preoccupied with Iceland's exotic natural phenomena, are worth seeking out in Reykjavik, as are the sculptures of **Einar Jónsson** (d. 1954) and **Ásmundur Sveinsson**.

Architecture Until recent times, Scan-dinavian architecture followed in the wake of the rest of Europe, with local variations – the most striking example from early times is the medieval stave church of Norway, with its multiple rooflets adorned with dragons' heads strongly reminiscent of Viking figureheads. For a long time, timber was the main building material and whole towns were destroyed by fire with un-fortunate regularity. Rather early, how-ever, the Danes learned how to make bricks which became the principal build-ing material in that country. Gradually throughout the area wooden houses, churches and fortifications were replaced by more enduring stone, and the successive influences of Gothic, Renais-sance, Baroque and Rococo filtered northwards.

Around the turn of the century, there was a passionate flourishing of National Romantic styles, especially in Finland which was restlessly establishing its own identity under Czarist rule. Leading names from that period are **Lars Sonck** (1870–1956), **J.S. Siren** (1889–1961) and, most prolific of all, **Eliel Saarinen** (1873–1950) who designed Helsinki Railway Station and town halls all over Finland. It was about the same time that **Ragnar Östberg** was creating Stockholm's imposing City Hall, and a few years later that **Magnus Poulsson** and **Arnstein Arneberg** began work on that of Oslo; both buildings house major contributions from the artists of each country.

The paramount feature of Scandinavia's modern architecture is the successful combination of grace, function and harmony with surrounding nature. There are many outstanding examples created by a considerable list of leading architects in each country, but undoubtedly the most famous name of all remains Finland's **Alvar Aalto** (d. 1976) whose schools, homes and public buildings are dotted around the world, as well as many parts of his native land.

PAPERWORK

(See also If you are Motoring, p. 16) The whole area forms a passport-free zone which means that the citizens of any of these countries do not need passports to visit others within the area and non-Scandinavians need normally show their documents only on entering and leaving the zone. Visas are not required by British or North American visitors.

UK visitors A standard British passport (valid 10 years) is issued after application on the form obtainable at any main post office or from the Passport Offices in London, Liverpool, Peterborough, Glasgow and Newport, Gwent. Residents of Northern Ireland should apply in person to the Foreign and Commonwealth Office, Passport Agency, 30 Victoria St., Belfast BT1 3LY, or by post to the Passport Office, Empire House, 131 West Nile St., Glasgow G1 2RY. Two regulation photographs and proof of identity, plus endorsement by a person of standing are required. British Visitor's Passports are also valid for periods not exceeding three months in any nine-month period. The completed BVP application form should be taken by the applicant to a main post office in England, Scotland or Wales (*not* mainland Passport Offices), or the Passport Agency (address above) in Northern Ireland.

US visitors United States citizens whose last US passport was issued within the past 8 years and after their 18th birthday may apply by mail to their nearest Passport Agency for a new passport. US Domestic Passport Agencies are located in: Boston, Chicago, Detroit, Honolulu, Houston, Los Angeles, Miami, New Orleans, Philadelphia, San Francisco, Seattle, Stamford and Washington. All others must appear personally at the nearest Passport Agency (parents may make applications on behalf of children under the age of 13). Each application must be accompanied by the applicant's latest US passport (or US birth certificate if no previous passport has been held), two identical regulation photographs and the passport fee.

Health There are no special requirements for visitors from the UK or North America, either on entering Scandinavia or on return to their own country. Within Scandinavia, the medical services are subsidized to various degrees and guidance is given on p. 26. If in doubt that you will be adequately covered, despite the moderate costs likely to be involved in case of need, the small premium required for insuring against risk of illness or injury is a wise investment. American visitors in particular should check that their health insurance policy covers them when abroad.

Insurance of property is also advisable; loss or theft should be reported to the police and a copy of the report obtained to satisfy your insurers.

CUSTOMS

The normal concession for UK visitors to Scandinavia (except Denmark) is 1 litre of spirits (Norway $\frac{3}{4}$ litre), 1 litre of wine, and 200 cigarettes or 250 grammes tobacco. Travellers resident in non-European countries may bring in double the quantity of tobacco. In the case of Denmark, which is a member of the European Economic Community, UK and other EEC residents may bring in 1$\frac{1}{2}$ litres of spirits, 3 litres of wine and 300 cigarettes or 400 grammes tobacco. A special facility in Iceland is that you may buy duty-free goods at Keflavik International Airport on entering as well as leaving the country. Note that the minimum age for bringing spirits into Scandinavia is 20 years (Denmark 17 years).

Every country has its list of restricted goods, few of which are likely to affect the law-abiding visitor. If you are on a self-catering holiday, note that for most of the area you may bring in up to 15 kilos of food per person, which should not include fresh, frozen or smoked meat or fish. You are safe with all forms of tinned goods as well as tea, coffee, dried soups and vegetables, cereals, sugar and biscuits. Some restrictions (such as dried milk in the case of Norway) are rather unexpected so, if in doubt, check.

There is a fairly high sales tax throughout Scandinavia, which can be avoided under certain circumstances on major purchases (see p. 27–8). The chart below indicates what travellers may bring home free of duty.

Duty-free allowances *subject to change*		Goods bought in a duty-free shop	Goods bought in EEC
Tobacco	Cigarettes *or*	200	300
	Cigars *small* *or*	100	150
	Cigars *large* *or*	50	75
	Pipe tobacco	250 gm	400 gm
Alcohol	Spirits *over 38.8° proof* *or*	1 litre	1½ litres
	Fortified or sparkling wine *plus*	2 litres	3 litres
	Table wine	2 litres	4 litres
Perfume		50 gm	75 gm
Toilet water		250 cc	375 cc
Other goods		£28	£120

(note in box at left of Tobacco row:) Double if you live outside Europe

US customs permit duty-free $300 retail value of purchases per person, 1 quart of liquor per person over 21, and 100 cigars per person.

CURRENCY

Travellers' checks are the safest. From May, 1983, British travellers wanting to use their cheque books overseas will have to apply to their bank for a separate Eurocheque card to present with their cheques at European banks. Although accepted in many places, indicated by display, international credit cards are not so widely used, especially in Iceland and Norway, as in some other parts of the world. The units of currency and normal banking hours for each country are given below, but much longer hours apply to international airports, main railway stations, harbours and certain exchange bureaus in main cities, while in rural areas the hours may be much more restricted. Money can usually also be exchanged in hotels or at local tourist offices (except Finland) outside banking hours, though the rate given will often be a little lower and, especially in Finnish and Swedish hotels, substantially so. Reasonable amounts of local currency can be taken out of each of the countries, but if large sums

are involved you should check current regulations. **Denmark** 1 krone, plural kroner, divided into 100 øre. Banks open 0930–1600 Mon.–Fri. (0930–1800 Thurs. in Copenhagen); closed Sat. **Finland** 1 markka, plural markkaa, divided into 100 penniä. Banks open 0930–1600 Mon.–Fri.; closed Sat. **Iceland** 1 króna, plural krónur, divided into 100 aurar. Banks open 0915–1600 Mon.–Fri.; closed Sat. Because of Iceland's high inflation rate it is not advisable to buy krónur until you need them. **Norway** 1 krone, plural kroner, divided into 100 øre. Banks open 0800/0815–1500/1530 Mon.–Fri. (0800/0815–1700/1800 on Thurs. in main cities); closed Sat. **Sweden** 1 krona, plural kronur, divided into 100 öre. Banks open 0930–1500 Mon.–Fri. (0930–1700/1800 on Thurs. in main cities); closed Sat.

HOW TO GET THERE

National tourist boards provide a list of tour operators featuring their countries. A selection of specialists is given on p. 29, but the situation is subject to change.

By Air The only country imposing a separate airport tax is Iceland and this is fairly high. Note that there are many reduced return fare variations, such as Apex, Excursion, Eurobudget, and the current situation should be checked. Regular services are far too numerous to be listed, but the following airlines provide direct links. **From the US** Finnair, Icelandair, Northwest Orient, SAS. Note the advantageous stop-over arrangements in Iceland when travelling between the US and Europe. **From the UK** The main operators are British Airways, Finnair, Icelandair and SAS; in addition, Air UK and Dan-Air have services to Norway, including flights out of a number of provincial airports. Many other services link the principal cities of Europe with Scandinavia.

By Sea Direct routes are as follows: **Denmark** Harwich or Newcastle–Esbjerg, year round, 19 hours (DFDS Danish Seaways); Scrabster (Scotland)–Tórshavn (Faroes), summer only, 15 hours (Faroese Coastal Service). **Finland** Tilbury–Helsinki, infrequently, 3 days (Baltic Shipping Co.). **Iceland** Scrabster (Scotland)–Seydisfjördur (east coast), summer only, 35 hours (Faroese Coastal Service). **Norway** Newcastle–Stavanger/Bergen, summer only, 18/20 hours (DFDS Danish Seaways); Newcastle–Oslo, summer only, 26 hours (DFDS Danish Seaways). **Sweden** Felixstowe–Gothenburg, year round, 23 hours (DFDS Tor Line); Newcastle–Gothenburg, summer only, 25 hours (DFDS Tor Line).

Note that some of these services can be used in conjunction with onward travel to neighbouring countries by means of the inter-Scandinavian ferries mentioned on p.15. This also applies to DFDS Prins Ferries year-round services from Harwich to Bremerhaven/Hamburg (North Germany), 16/20 hours, which can be used in conjunction with Finnlines services from Travemünde to Helsinki (22 hours). If you are travelling through Germany, you should check other services linking North Germany with several Scandinavian ports.

There are no direct passenger sailings from North America to Scandinavia.

By Road/Sea All the services listed above carry cars. Under certain conditions, usually if accompanied by four full fare-paying passengers, cars travel free on routes to Scandinavia and North Germany; bicycles are carried free on most routes, or for a nominal charge on the others. You can, of course, make use of the shorter sea crossings, such as Harwich–Hook of Holland (Sealink), Felixstowe–Zeebrugge (Townsend

Thoresen), Dover–Ostend (Sealink). There are no motorail services from Channel ports to Scandinavia.

There are no direct Europabus services to Scandinavia. It is possible to travel from London (Victoria Coach Station) via Cologne to Hamburg and from there on to Stockholm, but onward tickets can only be purchased in Germany. The Finnish bus company, Pohjolan Liikenne, operates a year-round service between Gothenburg and Helsinki using the Viking Line Stockholm–Turku route; this could be used in conjunction with North Sea services to Gothenburg.

By Rail The Eurail Pass (1st and 2nd class) and Eurail Youthpass (for under-26s, 2nd class only) are valid for unlimited rail travel in most European countries (including Scandinavia), but can only be purchased outside Europe. Valid for one month of unlimited rail travel in most European countries (but excluding the issuing country) are the fixed-price Inter-Rail Youth Card for under-26s and Inter-Rail Senior Pass for men over 65 and women over 60; holders are also entitled to big reductions on many cross-Channel services. The Youth Card can be bought in the UK, but not the Senior Pass. (See also p. 15.)

The principal routes are as follows; advance bookings and seat reservations are necessary. **Denmark** London (Liverpool St. Station)–Harwich–Esbjerg–Copenhagen, 27 hours; Newcastle–Esbjerg–Copenhagen, 25 hours; London (Liverpool St. Station)–Harwich–Hook of Holland–Copenhagen, 23 hours; London (Victoria Station)–Dover–Ostend–Copenhagen, 22 hours. **Finland** As for Copenhagen or Stockholm, and then by one of several ferries (see p. 15), 2–3 days. **Norway** As for Copenhagen and then, via Helsingør–Helsingborg–Gothenburg, 10 hours to Oslo. **Sweden** As for Copenhagen and then, via Helsingør–Helsingborg, 8 hours to Stockholm, or 5 hours to Gothenburg.

INTERNAL TRAVEL

An extremely varied transport network exists to link communities across the considerable distances and often difficult terrain of Scandinavia. All the national tourist boards provide full information; in particular those of Finland and Norway publish summaries combining details of main routes on all forms of transport.

Air In Denmark, Norway and Sweden, domestic services are operated by SAS in cooperation with smaller airlines (Danair in Denmark, Braathens-SAFE in

Norway, Linjeflyg in Sweden); in Finland by Finnair, and in Iceland by Icelandair. An ever-changing variety of reductions applies to domestic and inter-Scandinavian fares and it is essential to check the latest situation. Note that some of these apply only if tickets are bought outside Scandinavia; others only if bought within the area. As a guide, reductions are likely to apply in the following circumstances: (1) if you travel on off-peak flights to some destinations; (2) if you are a family group with one or more children under 26; (3) if you are under 22–25 years (depending on country); (4) if you are not less than 60–67 years (depending on country).

The following specific concessions also apply: **Denmark** free onward travel from Copenhagen within Denmark if the ticket were bought before leaving the UK, provided there is no break of journey in Copenhagen. **Finland** unlimited travel for 15 days using the fixed-price Finnair Holiday Ticket. **Iceland** reductions on round-Iceland and triangular trips; also air/bus combinations.

Rail For international rail passes, see p. 14. In addition, there is the fixed-price Nordic Railpass valid throughout Denmark, Finland, Norway and Sweden for 21 days or 1 month of unlimited travel (1st or 2nd class), also giving 50 per cent reductions on many inter-Scandinavian shipping services. In all four countries, families of three or more qualify for reductions when travelling together. Children travel half price or free, but the age range varies according to country. There are also discounts for over-65s in many cases. Other concessions are as follows, but as these are liable to change, you should check the current situation as well as any special excursion fares which may apply on specific journeys. **Denmark** Fixed-price Take-Five tickets give unlimited travel for any 5 days within a 17-day period on Danish State Railways services, including some ferries and buses. **Finland** The fixed-price Finnrail Pass gives unlimited travel for 8, 15 or 22 days and is available to foreigners on showing their passports. Tourist tickets combined with other forms of travel also give reductions, but must be booked ahead. **Iceland** No railways! **Norway** Reductions on one-way journeys on several days of the week allow breaks of journey and are especially worthwhile on long journeys. Combined rail/bus tours offer very good rates detailed in the *Selected Cheap Circular Tours* folder from Norwegian State Railways. **Sweden** Swedish State Railways have achieved the miracle of reducing big losses by completely re-thinking their fare structure which now includes remarkable bar-

gains. For a very reasonable outlay, the *Lågpriskort* (low-priced card) entitles you to huge reductions on all rail journeys within Sweden, year round and any day except Fridays and Sundays.

Bus This is the best method of travel for getting in touch with the countryside; in many areas it is the only one. In all cases there are reductions for children. **Denmark** Bus services operated by Danish State Railways (DSB) are covered by the Take-Five ticket (above). **Finland** There is an intensive network of regular and express (small additional charge) bus services, supplemented by the mail-carrying yellow postbuses that reach the remotest areas. Over-65s can buy the special 65 Card (photo and passport needed) entitling them to considerable reductions. There is also a Tourist Ticket valid for 7 days unlimited travel on express coaches (excluding Lapland). **Iceland** The fixed-price Omnibus Passport entitles you to unlimited travel by scheduled services for periods of one week to one month. The Full-Circle Passport provides the freedom of a trip round Iceland without time limit. There are also air/bus combinations. **Norway** Bus services are privately run on a regional basis and usually take over where rail or boat services stop. They form part of the *Selected Cheap Circular Tours* (above). Reduced fares apply to over-67s. **Sweden** Express and regular bus services are supplemented by the mail-carrying yellow postbuses which penetrate the remotest areas. Special excursion tickets give good rates in certain regions. Over-65s get reductions.

Ferries (see also Inland and coastal waters, below) Scandinavia has probably the most intensive and efficient network of drive-on drive-off ferries of any area in the world. Below is a summary of the inter-Scandinavian routes, but check the latest situation. **Denmark–Faroes** Esbjerg–Tórshavn (DFDS Danish Seaways); Hanstholm–Tórshavn (Faroese Coastal Service). **Denmark–Finland** Copenhagen–Helsinki (Finnlines). **Denmark–Norway** Copenhagen–Oslo (DFDS Danish Seaways); Frederikshavn–Oslo (DA-NO Linjen, Stena Line); Frederikshavn–Larvik (Larvik Line); Hanstholm–Kristiansand (Skagerak Expressen); Hirtshals–Arendal (Skagerak Expressen); Hirtshals–Kristiansand (Skagerak Expressen). **Denmark–Sweden** Copenhagen–Malmö (Öresundslinjerne); Dragør–Limhamn (Öresundslinjerne); Frederikshavn–Gothenburg (Stena Line, Sessan Tor Line); Grenå–Helsingborg (Lion Ferry); Grenå–Varberg (Lion Ferry); Helsingør–Helsingborg (Swedish State Railways, LB-färjorna); Rønne

(Bornholm)–Ystad (Carl Gram). **Faroes–Iceland** Tórshavn–Seydisfjördur (Faroese Coastal Service). **Finland–Sweden** Helsinki–Slite (Finnlines); Helsinki–Stockholm (Silja Line, Viking Line); Jakobstad (Pietarsaari)–Skellefteå (Jakob Lines); Mariehamn (Åland)–Kapellskär (Viking Line); Naantali–Mariehamn–Kapellskär (Viking Line); Turku–Mariehamn–Stockholm (Silja Line, Viking Line); Vaasa–Sundsvall Wasaferry); Vaasa–Umeå (Wasaferry). **Norway–Faroes** Bergen–Tórshavn (Faroese Coastal Service).

The following guidelines apply within each country. **Denmark** There are 45 domestic ferries, a number of them operated by Danish State Railways, with various possibilities for combining connecting crossings for through-tickets, or return tickets valid for alternative services. Car fares usually include the driver. Off-season fares are lower and quite a few special offers apply on certain routes at certain times. A free leaflet *Car Ferries*, revised annually, is available from the Danish Tourist Board listing all domestic and international services. **Finland** South west Finland is linked with the Åland islands as follows: Turku–Mariehamn (Silja Line, Viking Line); Naantali–Mariehamn (Viking Line). **Sweden** There are regular links with Visby (Gotland) from Nynäshamn, Västervik, Oskarshamn and Grankullavik (Öland).

Inland and coastal waters (see also Ferries, above) **Finland** Many regular services and cruises in summer on Finland's labyrinthine waterways offer possibilities ranging from a few hours by hydrofoil or motorship to one- to seven-day cruises, sleeping on board or in port, picking up another boat a day or more later. Meals and refreshments are available on board and in many cases cars are transported between terminals. The season is normally from late May to late August and main routes are on the Saimaa lake system; Päijänne (Lahti–Jyväskylä); the Silver Line route (Hämeenlinna–Tampere); Poet's Way route (Tampere–Virrat). Waterbus trips operate out of Turku to coastal and island communities. Cruises also offer the opportunity to visit the Soviet Union from Helsinki, Lappeenranta or Kotka. **Iceland** A cargo-passenger service operates clockwise and anticlockwise round Iceland, but no advance timetable is published and details must be checked in Reykjavík. **Norway** An 11-day round trip Bergen–Kirkenes–Bergen via the North Cape operates year round with almost daily departures, calling at several ports each day. It can be done in sections or in its entirety providing an unforgettable cruise. There are also many shorter fjord cruises and an intensive network of regular ferry services in all the fjord districts, linking like clockwork with bus or rail services, through often spectacular scenery. The principal inland waterway routes are on the Telemark Canal and Lake Mjøsa. **Sweden** The famous Göta Canal (p. 99) links Gothenburg and Stockholm in three days by motorship. Other regular summer services are on Lakes Vättern and Siljan and on the Dalsland Canal. From Gothenburg and especially Stockholm sightseeing boats and regular ferries link the cities with extensive archipelagoes.

Taxis A roof sign 'Taxi' is lit when the vehicle is free. Charges are fairly high and, except in Denmark, there is an additional charge in the evening or at night and, in some cases, at weekends. See also Tipping (p. 28).

Organized excursions During the summer there is a wide variety from all main cities and resorts, but at other times organized sightseeing is limited to the capitals and one or two main cities. With advanced planning, combination tickets using various forms of public transport, according to season, offer plenty of year-round possibilities.

IF YOU ARE MOTORING

Driving in Scandinavia is mostly untaxing and traffic is light (at times nonexistent!) except near main cities or resorts at holiday times. Allow plenty of time for covering long distances through often rugged country. Members of their own national motoring organizations may find they can take advantage of certain extra facilities offered by those in Scandinavia (see Useful Addresses, p. 29).

Documents UK visitors taking their own car will need their British driving licence (not a provisional) plus, in Iceland, an International Driving Permit; car registration certificate; an oval national identity sticker (GB or equivalent); and insurance certificate. Though the International Green Card of Insurance is no longer compulsory, it is highly recommended and may save inconvenience in the case of accident. It can be obtained from your insurance company by paying a small extra premium. You should, in any case, check that your insurance cover is adequate for your needs, including damage while in transit.

US visitors are advised to have an International Driving Permit for Finland and Iceland.

Rules of the Road

You drive on the right and give way to traffic from the right unless it is clearly marked that you have priority. This also applies to traffic on roundabouts. Trams (and their passengers) always have priority. Pedestrians at official crossing places have right of way over traffic, including filter traffic.

Road standards Free maps from the national tourist boards clearly mark major and minor roads. In **Denmark**, all roads are asphalted and well maintained. There are quite a few stretches of motorway and no toll charges; however, remember there are many ferries and costs can quickly mount up. In **Finland**, **Norway** and **Sweden**, main and many secondary roads are excellent. In the far north and remoter areas, surfaces may be oil-gravel or gravel but well maintained. Take special care in the spring thaw when some roads are closed for a time and some sections may be pitted with potholes. In **Norway** especially, many mountain roads are closed in winter, sometimes until late into spring. There are few stretches of motorway except near some main cities and no toll charges, except on the Oslo–Drammen motorway in Norway and a number of minor roads in the Norwegian mountains. Short river-ferry crossings are usually free, but on longer journeys, especially through the fjord systems of Norway, fares, though heavily subsidized, can mount up. In **Iceland**, very few stretches of road are asphalted.

Road signs These are mostly international and easy to follow. In **Finland**, **Norway** and **Sweden**, unusual hazards are elk or reindeer on the roads (depicted pictorially) and encounters have resulted in nasty accidents especially at dusk. In **Iceland** the hazard is more likely to be cattle, horses and especially sheep.

Lights Headlights for left-hand traffic must be adapted with some opaque material. During the day, dipped headlights must be used in poor light, mist or fog in **Denmark**, **Iceland** and **Norway**; additionally at all times from 1 September to 30 April outside built-up areas in **Finland** regardless of conditions, and in all circumstances, year round, in **Sweden**.

Safety (see also Lights, above). The carrying of a warning triangle, the use of seat belts by drivers and front-seat passengers, and the wearing of crash helmets by motorcyclists are compulsory throughout the area (except Iceland). The use of the horn is only permitted in order to avert danger; headlights should be flashed instead.

Breakdowns The general recommendation in the many sparsely populated areas is to stop the next car for assistance in reaching a garage or telephone. Any breakdown service received must be paid for. For emergency numbers see p. 26. **Denmark** There are emergency telephones on motorways at frequent intervals. If you cannot drive to a garage, call FALCK, the nationwide salvage corps. **Finland** There are emergency telephones on main roads. Autoliitto (Automobile and Touring Club of Finland, ACTF) operates a road patrol service (vehicles carry a yellow roof sign). **Iceland** The Icelandic Motoring Club (FIB) operates patrols at weekends in summer. **Norway** There are many emergency telephones on main roads and in mountain areas, and limited road patrols operated by the Norwegian Motoring Club (NAF) in summer. NAF also runs a 24-hour breakdown service through local garages, though it may be quicker to contact one of the latter direct. **Sweden** Emergency telephones on main roads are limited. A 24-hour service is operated by Larmtjänst (Alarm Services), a central breakdown organization run by insurance companies. There is also a 24-hour emergency garage service in most towns.

Spares and repairs Servicing and minor repairs can be carried out in most places and major repairs in towns. There may, however, be difficulty in getting spares for cars of British make in Norway and Sweden. It can be worth renting a spares kit from your motoring organization or garage, who should also be able to rent out warning triangles and emergency windscreens. A set of spare bulbs should be carried. The following additional items are recommended by the Automobile Association: a pair of windscreen wiper blades, a length of electrical cable, an inner tube of the correct type, a roll of insulating or adhesive tape, a torch, a fire extinguisher, and a tow rope.

Speed limits: Denmark 60kph/37mph in built-up areas, otherwise 80/50 on the open road or 100/62 on motorways; maximum for trailers 70/43. **Finland** 50kph/31mph in built-up areas; otherwise 60/37, 80/50, 110/68 or 120/74 as indicated. If not indicated, the basic limit is 80/50, which is also the maximum for trailers. **Iceland** 40kph/25mph in built-up areas, otherwise 70/43. **Norway** 50kph/31mph in built-up areas, 80/50 on the open road, 90/56 on motorways; maximum for trailers 70/43 with brakes, 60/37 without brakes. **Sweden** 30kph/19mph in school areas, 50/31 in built-up areas; otherwise 70/43, 90/56 or 110/68 as indicated. Maximum for trailers 70/43 with brakes, 40/25 without brakes.

Drinking and driving The law is very

strict, the penalties for breaking it severe and there are many spot checks. The legal maximum throughout is $0.5^o/_{oo}$ of alcohol in the blood, except in Denmark where it is $0.8^o/_{oo}$; less in the case of accident. In short, if you drink don't drive.

Parking Look out for signs incorporating the word *forbudt* or *förbud*, meaning prohibited. Parking is only a problem in a few main cities. Sometimes restrictions apply on even/uneven dates or to house numbers so, if in doubt, check. If restrictions are ignored, the car may be towed away or a heavy fine imposed. **Denmark** Limited waiting is always indicated on signs, and parking discs are then required (available from filling stations, post offices, some banks); otherwise use a parking meter or multistory car park. **Finland** There are meters and a few multistory car parks. **Iceland** There are meters, but parking is rarely a problem. **Norway** Parking is mainly on meters, also a few multistory parks. **Sweden** There are meters and multistory parks; parking is relatively easy but expensive.

Fines Speeding and parking offences are the most common and speed checks are rather frequent. In **Denmark**, on-the-spot fines are imposed and, if not paid, the car may be impounded. In **Finland**, **Norway** and **Sweden** you are given a ticket which must be paid at a post office.

Tyres Remember that your tyres must still meet the legal requirements at the end of your journey and, if in doubt, replace them. If you are travelling in winter, spiked or studded tyres may be used normally from early or mid October to mid or late April, according to area (rarely required in Denmark). Spiked tyres must be fitted to all wheels. Chains may be necessary if tyre equipment is not adequate for winter conditions.

Vehicle width The normal maximum is 2.5m/8ft 2in. The exception is in **Norway** where it is 2.35m/7ft 8¾in for cars and 2.2m/7ft 3in for trailers (caravans). If your trailer does not conform to this rule, you should apply for a special permit to Vegdirektoratet (Roads Directorate), PO Box 8109, Oslo 1. This office publishes a leaflet *With trailers on tow on Norwegian roads* available from the Norwegian Tourist Board.

Fuel In **Denmark** (except on motorways) and in the more populated southern regions of **Finland**, **Norway** and **Sweden**, filling stations are plentiful. In the remoter areas and **Iceland**, it is highly advisable to keep your tank topped up. The grades normally available are 92/93, 96 and 98/99 octane, except in Iceland where fuel, imported from the Soviet Union, is never higher than 94 octane.

Some garages, especially in Denmark and Sweden, use automats for which you will need bank notes of certain denominations.

Accidents See also Breakdowns, above, and p. 26 for emergency numbers. If you are involved in an accident, you must stop. Place a warning triangle on the road at an effective distance and seek medical assistance for any injured persons. If required by law, report to the police, leave the vehicle where it is and make sure that all essential particulars are noted. Should it be causing a serious obstruction, mark its position before independent witnesses. If possible, take a photograph of the scene. Check your insurance policy and notify the company within 24 hours in writing. **Denmark** Exchange details with anyone else involved and contact the police. If you are wholly or partly responsible, get in touch with Dansk Forening for International Motorkøretøjsforsikring, Amaliegade 10, 1256 Copenhagen K. **Finland** It is a legal requirement to seek medical help if necessary; if you do not, you are liable to prosecution. Before major repairs, report to Liikennevakuutusyhdistys (Finnish Motor Insurers' Bureau), Bulevardi 28, Helsinki 12. **Iceland** Report to the police in the nearest community; a passing motorist will invariably stop and give you a lift. **Norway** The only firm rule is that, in the case of injury, medical assistance must be obtained and the police called. **Sweden** It is not obligatory (though advisable in your own interests) to call the police, but you are legally required to give your name and address to other persons concerned before leaving the scene of the accident, however slight. Failure to do so makes you liable to prosecution.

Car rental This is widely available, usually at main airports, railway stations and through international or local firms (the latter may be cheaper). It can also be arranged in advance through tour operators specializing in Scandinavia.

Car-carrying trains These operate on the following routes: **Finland** Helsinki–Oulu/Rovaniemi and Turku/Tampere–Rovaniemi; **Norway–Sweden** Narvik–Kiruna.

WHERE TO STAY

There is no official classification of **hotels**, but standards are high. Annually revised lists of hotels and, in most cases, all other forms of accommodation, are distributed free by the national tourist boards. These lists give details of the amenities of each establishment as well as prices, clearly showing whether local taxes, service, *etc*, are included. Central accommodation-booking offices are maintained, usually in main railway stations, with long opening hours throughout summer. Local tourist offices will always assist with advice and, often, make bookings.

A Bonus Passport scheme of vouchers offering 20–40 per cent reductions in many first-class hotels in Denmark, Finland, Norway and Sweden operates from mid June to end August, and can be purchased through several UK agents. Other schemes are mentioned under each country below, but the latest situation should be checked with each national tourist board. In many cases, there are reductions for children sharing parents' room. Full- or half-board terms usually apply to minimum stays of 3 to 5 days. Two other types of establishment common to much of the Nordic area are the Mission Hotels, run by religious organizations, usually of good standard though mainly unlicensed; and Summer Hotels, using school or university accommodation, which is normally modern, functional, and often run by the students.

Note that **youth hostels** in the Nordic countries are open to all age groups, but you are usually required to be a member of your national or the international youth hostel association, or to take out temporary membership on the spot. Sleeping bags are not usually allowed (except in Iceland) so you will need a sheet sleeping bag (which can sometimes be rented).

Campsites in the Nordic countries are classified according to a one- to three-star system. Usually you are required to hold an international FICC camping card (not in Norway), or you may take out a national camping card on the spot. On many sites, though to a lesser extent in Finland and the remoter parts of Norway, there are electricity and sometimes water and mains sewage link-ups to trailers (caravans). Many sites also offer accommodation in huts or chalets.

An often misunderstood feature of the Nordic countries is 'all-man's-right' by which free use of the countryside is available to all, especially in Finland, Norway and Sweden. This right, alas, has been abused by some visitors and, as a result, 'wild' camping is often discouraged and may arouse mistrust in some localities. Basically the 'right' entitles you to walk across or pitch your tent (but not trailer) on uncultivated land, at least 150m/160yd from any habitation, though you should not stay longer than two days without consent of the landowner except in remoter areas. You are, of course, expected to cause no damage, leave no rubbish and to observe all the normal

courtesies of quiet and orderly behaviour. Camp fires are normally strictly prohibited.

If you are using butane gas, please note that bottles may be refilled or replaced only in a *very* few places at present and you are strongly advised to bring sufficient supplies or to check current availability with the national tourist boards. Alternatively, inexpensive, expendable bottles of other liquid petroleum gas are available for attachment to camping equipment sold in the Nordic and most other European countries.

Denmark Inter DK Hotels is an association of independent first-class hotels and White House Hotels a chain of top establishments. A characteristic feature of the Danish scene is the *kro* (inn), often a charming, half-timbered building offering traditional decor and food. Many take part in the economical Danish Inn Holiday Scheme: vouchers are valid at any of those participating, and available through the central booking office of Dantourist (address p. 29). Particularly well organized are the farmhouse holidays, now established many years, offering full- or half-board accommodation on working farms all over the country. Visitors normally eat with the family and often participate in activities about the farm. It is an ideal holiday for those with children, travelling by car. Stays are usually for a minimum of one week and can be booked, including travel arrangements, through Danish Seaways and other UK tour operators (addresses p. 29). There are also plenty of opportunities for self-catering either in small individual cottages or in holiday centres which combine apartments or cottages with restaurant and recreational facilities. Accommodation in private houses is available, usually through local tourist offices. You can get a free list of youth hostels from the Danish Tourist Board, which also includes most campsites, of which there are 500 approved by the National Camping Commission. A detailed campsite guide can be bought locally.

Finland A hotel cheque scheme called Finncheque operates in about 150 hotels of various categories throughout the country from 1 June to 31 August; details are given in a leaflet from the Finnish Tourist Board. Several hotel groups, such as Polar Hotels, Point Hotels, Rantasipi Hotels and Scanhotels, may offer special packages. Inexpensive accommodation is available in a limited number of boarding houses (*matkustajakoti*) bookable through the central accommodation-booking office in Helsinki railway station or local tourist offices. The latter may also have details of limited private accommodation. Farmhouse holidays, with full- or half-board, are becoming increasingly popular and are described in a separate free leaflet. This also applies to self-catering accommodation in summer cottages and holiday villages, mostly idyllically situated by a lake or seashore amid the forests. You can choose an inexpensive cottage with very basic amenities or a sophisticated log cabin with every modern facility. A free leaflet lists both the 140 youth hostels and 340 campsites. Youth hostels are often in empty schools, and meals are not usually provided, though refreshments are often available and, in some, self-service kitchens.

Iceland There are several top-class hotels in Reykjavik. Outside the capital, many establishments belong to the chain of Edda hotels, mostly adapted into summer hotels from modern boarding schools. Least expensive in towns are boarding houses and private rooms. Farmhouse holidays are becoming popular. A few youth hostels and a score of other places offer cheap accommodation to those with sleeping bags. The 20 campsites are mostly fairly basic; otherwise, with a few exceptions (marked *Tjaldstaeði bönnud* – camping forbidden), you may camp almost anywhere on uncultivated or unfenced land, though near farms permission should be sought.

Norway Inter Nor is an association of first-class hotels, and there are several other groups at times offering advantageous packages. Hotels are supplemented by various other establishments such as the guest house (*pensjonat*); tourist hostel (*turistheim*) which normally offers fairly simple accommodation, sometimes with communal kitchen facilities; and mountain lodge (*fjellstue*), usually less elaborate than a hotel though increasingly offering similar standards. Private rooms are best outside main towns and may provide cooking facilities. Farmhouse holidays with full board are becoming popular. Self-catering chalets ranging from the extremely simple to the very well equipped are usually ideally situated for open-air holidays. In north Norway and especially the Lofotens, the *rørbu* (fisherman's shelter) has been adapted for those with a taste for the simple life, but you must bring all your own equipment. There is a free leaflet combining lists of youth hostels and campsites. Of over 100 hostels, some are of an exceptionally high standard; main ones offer full restaurant facilities, but not all have self-service kitchens. Of about 1400 campsites, 600 of the best are affiliated to the Norwegian Automobile Club (NAF; address p. 29)

who publish a separate, detailed free list.

Sweden A Swedish Hotel Cheque scheme operates in about 250 hotels in two different categories throughout the country from 1 May to 30 September (details in a leaflet from the Swedish Tourist Board). Some of the participating hotel chains, such as Inter S, Esso Motels, RESO, SARA and Sweden Hotels, may also offer their own separate packages. In addition to town and country hotels, other forms of accommodation include the guest house (*pensionat*), mountain hotel (*fjällstation*) and private room (*rum*). Farmhouses usually offer bed and breakfast, though some offer full board, and are booked through local tourist offices. Self-catering accommodation ranges from the simple and isolated cottage to well-equipped chalets in leisure centres with shops and sports facilities. A network of over 200 youth hostels (*vandrarhem*) is run by the Swedish Touring Club; standards are high. There is no free list, but an annual guide can be bought giving full details. A free list of campsites is issued by the Swedish Tourist Board from whom the much more detailed annual *Camping Book*, with over 550 sites, can be bought.

FOOD AND DRINK

Scandinavian family meal times are early. Lunch is from 1100/1200–1300/1400 and dinner 1600–1900, though hotel or restaurant evening meals are later – any time from 1800 or 1900. Within these time margins, the Finns and Norwegians eat the earliest, the Danes the latest. Most Scandinavians don't bother much with lunch and usually take sandwiches to their places of work, a fact that is reflected in the vast assortment of sandwiches available in snack bars and restaurants. The Scandinavian sandwich (Danish *smørrebrød*, Finnish *voileipä*, Norwegian *smørbrød*, Swedish *smörgås*) is in a class of its own. It is an open sandwich topped with an enormous choice of fish, meat, cheese, salad and different garnishes, decoratively arranged on a variety of breads. The talent for making food look attractive applies to all meals.

À la carte eating is expensive, but set meals at set prices between fixed hours bring costs down sharply. The Danes have introduced the Dan Menu, a two-course meal available in many restaurants throughout the country (list available from the Danish Tourist Board), and this trend towards tourist menus seems to be spreading. Service is always included (see Tipping, p. 28).

Breakfast is normally served from 0700/0730 onwards. Most hotels offer the choice of a continental breakfast, but the traditional Scandinavian breakfast is much more substantial. The Danes may include a delicious selection of sweet cakes or pastries, though some places now offer the extensive 'cold table' favoured in other parts of Scandinavia. If you travel by sea you will certainly get a good introduction to this gastronomic phenomenon, and it is such a major feature of Scandinavian eating that it requires some explanation.

The 'cold table' (Danish *koldt bord*, Finnish *voileipäpöytä*, Norwegian *koldtbord*, Swedish *smörgåsbord*) is literally a table bearing many different cold items from which you make your selection, returning as often as you like. The dishes reflect the rich harvests yielded by sea, river and lake, the game and fruits of the forests and mountains, as well as the more usual products of farm and market garden. The breakfast version is relatively modest; it will probably · include the much-loved salted herring, ham and possibly other cold meats, cheeses, tomatoes, eggs, cereals and different breads. There will be an inexhaustible supply of coffee, milk and various skimmed or sour milks, yoghurt, and tea (which a surprising number of Scandinavians prefer, even though it is invariably the tea-bag variety). It is quite sensible to stoke up at breakfast time and dispense with a big lunch.

The cold table at main meals is a majestic sight, groaning under the weight of dishes. Though there are variations from country to country, and from region to region, you are likely to come across most of the following items at some time or other: lobster, smoked or dill-cured salmon, smoked trout, prawns, shrimps, pickled or cured herring marinated or in a variety of sauces, fried Baltic herring (herring is particularly popular), smoked eel, thinly sliced roast beef, veal, pork, smoked reindeer meat, reindeer tongue, ham, liver pastes, tomatoes, onion rings, egg, pickled cucumber, gherkins, beetroot, and many preserves such as cranberry or red whortleberry. Cheeses include imitations of popular foreign kinds such as Stilton, Gruyère, Camembert, but there are also local varieties – Danish blue, sweet soft goat's cheese and even, if you are bold, the exceedingly strong *gamalost* ('old cheese') of Norway. All these are readily available in food shops and make tasty and inexpensive buys to take home. When it comes to desserts, the emphasis is on creamy soufflés, tiered cakes and a variety of soft fruits and berries, among which the greatest delicacy is the cloud-berry from the northern marshlands.

A gastronomic highlight of the Finnish and Swedish summer is the crayfish, a delicacy harvested from shallow streams and eaten in their thousands during a fixed period in July and August. Restaurants advertise special crayfish evenings and supply diners with decorative bibs as it's quite a messy business for the uninitiated. The crayfish are accompanied by aquavit, beer or white wine, so it is usually a convivial occasion too. In Denmark, Limfjord oysters are highly prized.

Many of the cold table ingredients are translated into delicious hot dishes. Salmon comes in many forms. Fillet of reindeer or young elk or ptarmigan in a cream sauce can be extremely good. Cream sauces are widely used, often incorporating the delicately flavoured mushrooms of which Scandinavia has many varieties. Among less expensive dishes are the ubiquitous spiced meatballs, pea soup with pork (traditionally followed by pancakes), and a whole range of fish such as cod, haddock, coalfish and mackerel. Norwegian *lutefisk* (cod steeped in a lye of potash) is definitely an acquired taste, as is Finland's *kalakukko* (fish and pork baked in a kind of pie). Icelandic specialities include smoked lamb (*hangikjöt*), dried fish (*hardfiskur*) and splendid curds (*skyr*). Potatoes are most often boiled, sometimes served with dill. Fresh vegetables are not so common, but a flourish of lettuce, tomato, beetroot, gherkin may well accompany a hot dish.

Coffee (usually strong, black or with cream) is drunk throughout Scandinavia; cold milk is also popular. Excellent lager-type beer of various strengths is widely available; the famous Danish beers are the best, but there are good ones throughout the area, except in Iceland whose beer is almost non-alcoholic. Local spirits are aquavit (*snaps*) and vodka of various kinds, though imported spirits are very popular (and very expensive). Imported wines, often bottled within each country, are relatively inexpensive. Some interesting liqueurs are distilled from the northern berries, notably from Arctic bramble, cloudberry and cranberry.

Licensing hours: Denmark Alcohol of all kinds is served at any time during opening hours, which are liberal. **Finland** Only beer is served before noon; after that all forms of alcohol are served until closing time. **Iceland** Only very mild beer is available; licensing hours for all forms of alcohol are 1200–1430 and 1900 to closing time, but no spirits at all are served on Wednesdays. **Norway** Beer or wine is available at any time; spirits are only available after 1500 (1300 in resort hotels), except for Sundays and on certain holidays, when beer or wine only is served. **Sweden** No alcohol is served before 1200 (1300 on Sundays) after which it is freely available until closing time.

Alcohol may be bought from many shops in Denmark; its sale in Finland, Iceland, Norway and Sweden, however, is a state monopoly. State monopoly shops are fairly widespread in Sweden and Finland, less so in Norway (there is a dearth in some resorts), and Iceland has very few. Beer is now also available in some supermarkets and cafeterias in Finland, Norway and Sweden.

Note the strict laws regarding drinking and driving (p. 17–18).

ENJOY YOURSELF

The best source for detailed information is always the national tourist board or local tourist office. The general information brochures published annually by each tourist board, for example, outline the facilities for many special interests; in addition, the Danish Tourist Board publishes annually a free booklet *Active Holidays*. Leaflets on individual sports are mentioned below and are free unless otherwise stated; many others are published by local tourist offices. Specialist firms marketing tours featuring some of these activities are listed on p. 29.

Bathing There is an enormous choice of sea- and lake-bathing, and though water temperatures may not match the Mediterranean, Nordic days can be warm, golden and up to 24 hours long, depending on latitude. There are vast stretches of sandy beach along the west coasts of Jutland, Sweden and Finland. But predominant in many areas of Finland, Norway and Sweden are the smooth granite rocks sloping gently down to lake or sea, ideal for walking and sunbathing on and swimming from. Another feature is space. Except for parts of the Danish coast and a handful of popular centres elsewhere in high season, seclusion is there for the asking. Outdoor and year-round indoor pools are common; many in Iceland are fed by natural thermal springs, making winter bathing a particular pleasure. A Danish Tourist Board map marks private and public beaches where nude bathing is practised; the Swedish Tourist Board can provide a list of many naturist clubs. In Finland nude bathing, an intrinsic part of the lake- or sea-side sauna (pp. 23, 53), is never 'mixed' in public saunas.

Canoeing This is a very popular sport in Scandinavia and canoes can be rented in many centres. Individual packages including rental of canoe and camping equipment are arranged, for example, in the Jutland lake district of Denmark, and through the Dalsland waterways of Sweden. There are guided trips, with rented equipment, through many remoter areas, such as central and eastern Finland, on Lake Femund in eastern Norway, and the Dalsland and Värmland districts of Sweden.

Cruising See Inland and coastal waters (p. 16)

Cycling Rental of cycles is widespread, and usually arranged through hotels or local tourist offices. Well-organized cycle packages for individuals are marketed by tourist offices, especially in Denmark (general booklet available) and Sweden (separate leaflets for Stockholm and various holiday areas); these usually include cycle rental, accommodation with half- or full-board, ferry tickets where necessary and detailed routes. Planned cycle routes are also available in parts of Finland. If you bring your own cycle, it travels free on some North Sea ferries.

Field Studies The best-organized guided tours for those interested in bird-watching, plants or geology, take place in Iceland which publishes several leaflets on its natural history. Otherwise there is good bird-watching in many coastal and mountain areas of Scandinavia, and many reserves can be visited (usually closed in the breeding season).

Fishing The varied waters and low level of pollution make Scandinavia a paradise for the fisherman. In all cases, local tourist offices should be consulted about permits and local regulations which can be quite complex. Broadly speaking, a local permit is required in all countries, plus a national permit in Finland and Norway for fresh-water fishing. Charges are normally very reasonable, though as elsewhere salmon fishing is expensive, if superlative, in some of the rivers of Iceland and northern Scandinavia. Denmark scores best for coarse fishing in Jutland. Fishing from the seashore is usually free, but a permit may be required. Stockholm is probably unique among capitals for the fishing from its bridges in the city centre, even resulting (though rarely) in salmon. Tackle can be rented from sports shops and some hotels; tackle imported into Norway must be disinfected. The following leaflets are useful: *Fishing* (Denmark), *Sports Fishing in Finland*, *Salmon and Trout Fishing in Iceland*, *Angling in Norway*, *Fishing in the Stockholm Region*.

Golf This is especially popular in Denmark (40 courses) and Sweden (140 courses). There are quite a few clubs in Finland, several near main towns in

Norway and a growing number in Iceland. Visitors are made very welcome.

Meeting the People There are limited schemes run by some tourist offices for visiting private homes for two or three hours on a non-commercial basis to exchange ideas; some advance notice is required. The scheme operates in Stockholm and in several Danish towns, but not Copenhagen.

Riding There are horse-riding schools throughout the area and sometimes arrangements can be made through hotels. In Norway, riding tours through the mountains are run by the Norwegian Mountain Touring Association (address p. 29). In Sweden, the best areas are Värmland and Dalarna. The sport is particularly popular in Iceland whose small sturdy horses, directly descended from their Viking Age ancestors, can be booked for day- or longer tours. They have their own special gait adapted to the rough terrain.

Sailing The fragmented coasts and scattered archipelagoes of Scandinavia offer superb sailing, as do some of the innumerable lakes. There are leaflets summarizing the regulations and amenities for those bringing their own vessels into Danish and Swedish coastal waters. No special restrictions apply, though you must, of course, comply with the customs regulations of each country. Bear in mind the strict rabies laws (p. 26). Rental of yacht or motor cruiser is quite widely available in Denmark and Sweden and, to a lesser extent, in Finland and Norway. There are also some sailing schools which arrange courses.

Sauna This remarkable cleansing and social institution originated in Finland where it remains an intrinsic part of the way of life (p. 53). It has spread widely especially throughout her Scandinavian neighbours, though the authentic Finnish article is rarely matched elsewhere. The experience is at its best in a lake- or seashore sauna when it can be combined with swimming and relaxation overlooking tranquil scenes. Contrary to popular belief, public saunas are never 'mixed'; there are certain hours for men or women, though most saunas can also be booked for private groups.

Tennis Available at many clubs, hotels campsites, *etc*, in Denmark, Norway and Sweden and, to a lesser degree, in Finland.

Walking and Climbing Few areas of the world offer wilder and more varied walking country and the amenities with which to enjoy it to the full. Be warned, however, that there are many areas of Finland, Iceland, Norway and Sweden

where you should *never* strike out alone unless you are fit, experienced and well equipped. Always ask for local advice and follow it, and always tell the hotel, hostel, campsite, *etc*, in which direction you are heading and when you intend to be back. Opportunities are endless and the following are only a few guidelines. **Denmark** Special events are the organized walks or marches in which many thousands participate each year. Most are for one day, but some are longer; the best known is a 2-day event from Viborg, in Jutland, in June. Longer walking tours with a guide include a 15-day route up Jutland's west coast. **Finland** An excellent booklet *Hiking Routes* outlines in English 24 marked trails throughout Finland ranging from 7–85km/4–53mi in length. **Iceland** Many guided treks and camping tours through parts of Iceland's extremely rugged interior are arranged, with camping equipment provided or available for rent. **Norway** There are over 20 mountain areas with cairned or marked trails and tourist chalets (with or without warden) spaced a day's walk apart. Unique are the self-service huts with blankets, food, wood, paraffin, and set charges (posted up inside) which you pay according to what you use. These provide truly remarkable possibilities for walking in remote mountain areas free of heavy packs. The huts are run by the very active Norwegian Mountain Touring Association (address p. 29), who can also supply all information on maps, guided tours, climbing and glacier courses, dog-sleigh touring in winter, *etc*. **Sweden** There is a number of marked long-distance trails (leaflet available) ranging from the King's Route in the far north (430km/266mi) passing Sweden's highest mountain Kebnekaise, to Sörmlandsleden, south of Stockholm, (500km/310mi, divided into 41 stages). One-day walks or full week hiking packages with guide and equipment are organized; details from the Swedish Touring Club (address p. 29).

Water Sports Rental of equipment and instruction in water skiing and windsurfing are widely available in Denmark and Sweden, and opportunities are increasing in Finland and Norway. (See also Bathing, Canoeing, Sailing.) Courses in skin diving are confined to Sweden's west coast.

Winter Sports Skiing as a sport was born in Scandinavia: in the Telemark district of Norway. And for several months of the year, Finland, Norway and Sweden become to a large extent nations on skis. Their national tourist boards produce excellent leaflets outlining amenities for visitors. Generally speaking, the gentle forested undulations and bare-topped fells of Finland and Sweden, or the grandiose highland plateaus of Norway are best suited to cross-country skiing and there are many marked trails. Cross-country equipment is much lighter than that used for downhill skiing and it can be rented or bought locally, usually inexpensively. In contrast, ski jumping is also very popular. Of recent years, ski lifts and tows have proliferated on the hills of all three countries, but Norway is by far the best developed in its facilities for downhill and slalom, and several resorts are featured in winter packages from the UK. Ski instruction and rental of equipment are available in all three countries. Nearly all centres provide illumination of some trails or slopes in the evening to counter-act the short daylight hours of midwinter. Après-ski entertainment tends to be more limited than in the Alpine countries, but there is always dancing in hotels or restaurants. Other winter activities include sleigh rides, fishing through holes in the ice, skidoo (motorized sledge) racing, and car racing on ice.

ENTERTAINMENT

Events of special note are mentioned throughout the gazetteer, and each national tourist board publishes a free calendar of events every year. One of the attractions of Scandinavia is the contrast between the modern amenities of even the smallest settlements and the often rugged nature, even isolation, of their settings. Until recent decades, communities had to make their own entertainment, and the many folk traditions that resulted survive to this day in pleasing contrast with the more sophisticated night life and cultural events of the cities. The seasons, too, whose rhythms play such an important part in much of Scandinavian life, are reflected in annual celebrations.

One example is May Day Eve, the Walpurgis Night of German legend called *Valbergsmässoafton* in Sweden and *Vapunaatto* in Finnish. This is as much as anything a welcome to the return of spring and a night, especially, for student pranks. Students and ex-students of all ages wear their graduation caps and splash about in fountains; balloons and other festive items are on sale; hotels and restaurants hold special dances and many people never see their beds this night. The festivities are most assiduously upheld in Finland and Sweden, the latter featuring huge bonfires in many places. Norway, on the other hand, goes to town on 17 May (Constitution Day). For the Danes 1 May means

the official opening of Tivoli and a sure sign that summer is on its way.

Huge bonfires in Denmark, most of Finland, Norway and northern Sweden signify Midsummer Eve, Scandinavia's other great ritual homage to the seasons – this time in honour of the year's longest day which, in the far north, is indeed 24 hours long. In Sweden and some western parts of Finland, the bonfire is replaced by a decorated maypole and this really old tradition, complete with folk dancing, music and feasting, is the most attractive of all (an especially lively time in the Swedish province of Dalarna). Again, few people see their beds this night. Mid-winter, too, has its celebrants, though only in Sweden where the Feast of St Lucia on 13 December features processions of the Queen of Light throughout the country – usually an attractive young lady wearing a crown of candles.

Because summer is relatively brief and to be enjoyed to the full, there is an emphasis on open-air entertainment. Nearly every town has its summer theatre with performances of national or foreign plays in the light Nordic evenings. The pleasure gardens in several cities of Denmark (notably Copenhagen's Tivoli) and Sweden (notably Gothenburg's Liseberg) are splendid places for family entertainment, ranging from full-scale funfairs and beautiful floral displays to top-class international shows with both popular and classical appeal: Open-air concerts of a high standard in city parks or the courtyards of castles and other historic buildings are many, sometimes even free. Street theatre and musicians proliferate in cities such as Copenhagen, Århus, Stockholm. An intriguing part of Sweden's town life are open-air chess and other games which attract small crowds of onlookers on any summer evening. Open-air markets cram the narrow streets of idyllic little towns in summer, but occur in winter, too, in main cities where they have their own special atmosphere as furred and booted stallholders stamp their feet in hard-packed snow, often against a backdrop of frozen harbour, with the winter sun a hazy orange ball low on the horizon.

Summer displays of folk dancing are numerous and there are many folk groups, often of professional standard, who maintain the traditions in each country. Though attractive regional costumes are no longer worn on an everyday basis, many are to be seen on festive occasions. The province of Dalarna in Sweden is particularly noted for its strong folkloric tradition, often reflecting the influence of the church, or the *mélange* of the pagan and Christian that is evident in much of rural Scandinavia. The colourful church boat processions of Dalarna are one example, another is the performance of allegorical plays, such as *The Road to Heaven* at Leksand. The mystery pageant *Petrus de Dacia* at Visby on the island of Gotland is a splendid spectacle. In Norway, too, there are many local events such as the peasant-style weddings in Voss and the children's weddings in the Hardangerfjord area, while the Fana folklore evenings arranged regularly throughout summer just outside Bergen are very popular.

In the far north, colourful Same (Lapp) festivals provide opportunities for scattered communities of these distinctive people to get together. Many of these occasions are church festivals, often held on Lady Day or at Easter when the snow is still thick on the ground and the full regalia of the Same costume, with its deep blues bordered with several bands of rich multicoloured braid, makes a splendid blaze of colour. Several weddings will probably take place at these times, as well as sporting events such as lasso-throwing competitions and reindeer races on some frozen lake. Important centres include Karasjok and Kautokeino in Norway, Inari and Enontekiö in Finland. There are also the big winter markets or fairs of the far north, usually in February or March, such as those of Jokkmokk and Arjeplog in Sweden. Denmark's traditional events tend to have a historical flavour. A major event is the Viking Festival in Frederikssund from mid June into early July. Tilting at the Ring festivities, with horse parades and competitions on horseback, are special features of south Jutland towns, especially Sønderborg.

There are several cultural festivals of a more conventional nature and of international standard, combining all kinds of music and drama. Leading events include the Bergen Festival, Helsinki Festival and Århus Festival. There are also many other important events. Jazz, for example, is the theme of an annual festival in Molde, Norway, the Pori Festival in Finland, and the Copenhagen Jazz Festival, while the Roskilde Festival (Denmark) is the biggest of its kind in northern Europe to focus on beat, jazz and folk music. A splendid medieval castle provides the setting for the Savonlinna Opera Festival in Finland, while mainly 18th-century operas unfold throughout summer in the exquisite Rococo theatre of Drottningholm, Stockholm. In Denmark, the children of Odense re-create the famous fairy tales for the Hans Christian Andersen Festival, and in Copenhagen the Theatre of Images fills the streets, parks, squares and open-air stages with mime, clowns, puppets, masks from all over the world. In Finland, two special themes are offered in the Kaustinen Folk Music Festival and the Lahti International Organ Festival. Folk songs are also the theme of the Skagen Ballad Festival in Jutland.

Though you would be misguided if you visited Scandinavia simply for its night life, conventional cabaret and discos abound in the big cities, with Copenhagen in the lead and Stockholm in second place. The popular places get crowded and you may find a burly doorman checking up on latecomers, probably gauging whether they appear desirable and/or properly dressed. This preoccupation with clothing (a tie is compulsory in some places) sometimes seems curiously at variance with the tolerance shown towards the drinking habits of the 'properly dressed' who have already gained entrance. The tendency of some Scandinavians towards over-indulgence in alcohol is a fact of life, though it is rarely intrusive in the better establishments. In tourist resorts and small towns, there is dancing on most nights in one hotel or more, quite often to a live band. This may be a dubious blessing if you want a quiet meal.

Other occasions when you are likely to see the Scandinavians letting down their hair are at major spectator sports events. There is fierce if friendly rivalry between them when it comes to sport, notably football and athletics in summer, and ice hockey, ski jumping and cross-country skiing in winter. Impressive spectacles of a gentler nature are the big sailing competitions (notably the round-Funen and round-Sealand regattas) of Denmark.

WHAT YOU NEED TO KNOW

Chemist Dispensing chemist's (pharmacies) are called *Apotek* in Denmark, Iceland (also *Lyfjaverslun*), Norway and Sweden. In Finland look for *Apteekki*. For normal hours see Opening Times (below), but all main towns will have at least one shop offering a 24-hour service. Your hotel, campsite or the local tourist office can give the address.

Churches Religious services in English are held in all the Scandinavian capitals, at least in summer, except for Iceland (at the Keflavik base only). Details of these and other services for all denominations are given in free local *What's On* publications or are available from local tourist offices; in Norway, services in English are also held in many tourist resorts.

Cigarettes and Tobacco   Foreign brands are readily available throughout the area, but are invariably expensive. Note that in Iceland, duty-free tobacco goods may be purchased on arrival at Keflavík Airport.

Electricity   With very few exceptions the current is 220 volts AC, 50 cycles, but you are likely to need an adaptor for the round 2-pin continental sockets.

Emergencies   Emergency telephone numbers for police, fire and ambulance are as follows: **Denmark** 000 nationwide; **Finland** 000 in Helsinki only; **Norway** 000 in Oslo only; **Sweden** 90 000 nationwide. Otherwise check in local directories or with your hotel, *etc.*

Health   There is some kind of reciprocal arrangement with Britain throughout the area, but North American visitors especially are advised to take out insurance cover, subject to the comments below, and, if you are on prescribed drugs, make sure you have sufficient supplies with you. Details of concessions for British visitors are given in Leaflet SA30 available from your local Department of Health and Social Security office or the DHSS Overseas Branch, Newcastle upon Tyne, NE98 1YX. In general these are as follows: **Denmark** In emergencies, hospital treatment for all foreigners is free; in other cases UK nationals also get free treatment, but North American visitors should expect to pay. UK nationals should show their passport to the doctor or chemist and, if payment is required, a refund can be obtained from the nearest municipal or health insurance office (address from tourist office). **Finland** Facilities for all foreigners are the same as for Finns, *ie* free use of health centres, a nominal daily charge for hospital inpatients, and a moderate charge for prescribed drugs. **Iceland** An Anglo-Icelandic agreement should be concluded by end 1982. In the meantime, emergency treatment is available to *all* visitors at a tiny nominal cost; otherwise they pay the same as the Icelanders. **Norway and Sweden** UK visitors are entitled to free treatment in hospitals (small nominal fee in Sweden) and part refund of doctor's fees as outpatients. Receipts should be taken with your UK passport to the local Social Insurance Office (*Trygdekasse* in Norway, *Försäkringskassan* in Sweden). Charges for prescribed drugs are moderate.

Note that, because of the risk of **rabies**, regulations throughout Scandinavia are extremely strict regarding the import of domestic pets which are subject to long quarantine (except those entering Denmark from the UK).

The UK totally prohibits the importation of animals (including domestic pets) except under licence. One of the conditions of the licence is that the animals are retained in approved quarantine premises for up to six months. No exemptions are made for animals that have been vaccinated against rabies. Penalties for smuggling involve imprisonment, unlimited fines and destruction of the animal.

Any animal being imported into the US must have a valid certificate of vaccination against rabies.

For further details apply to the Ministry of Agriculture (Animal Health Division), Hook Rise South, Tolworth, Surbiton, Surrey KT6 7NF.

Information   Local tourist offices in Scandinavia are usually exceptionally helpful and they offer a generous service which includes booking accommodation, arranging excursions and local package tours of general or special interest, changing money if the banks are closed, and generally directing your footsteps to the right source of information or help in almost any circumstance. Many of these offices publish annually revised leaflets, often in English, covering a wide range of local information. Tourist offices are usually identified by a small letter 'i', generally in white on a green background; otherwise look out for the following signs: **Denmark** *Turistbureau*; **Finland** *Matkailutoimisto*; **Norway** *Turist informasjon*; **Sweden** *Turistbyrå*.

Licensing Hours (see Food and Drink p. 21–2)

Lost Property   There are no central offices for all lost property – it depends where you lost it. The local tourist office will direct you to the police, railway, city transport office, *etc*, as relevant.

Mosquitoes   These can be a great nuisance, especially in the lake districts or in the far north, though much less so on the coast. Some summers are more afflicted than others, but the worst period is usually from midsummer to mid August. Repellents are not infallible, but they do help; seek advice from your chemist or doctor if you suffer from allergies.

Museums and Monuments   Throughout the area there are considerable variations in opening times within the range of 1000/1100–1500/1700 (or even later), so it is essential to check locally. Opening hours may be substantially shorter in winter and some museums close for that season. In summer most close one day a week, often Mon. Few museums are free (except in Iceland), but entrance fees compare favourably with those of the UK. Many, even in small towns and rural areas, display excellent explanatory texts in English, especially in Denmark and Norway, and in many cases guides in English can be bought though they can be quite expensive.

The concept of the open-air museum, re-creating communities of the past, comes from Scandinavia and many are well worth visiting. When it comes to monuments or other man-made traces from the past, Scandinavia scores high in Iron Age forts and burial mounds, mummified bodies, ship graves, prehistoric rock carvings, Viking remains, medieval churches, Renaissance castles and modern architecture. Further guidance is given throughout the gazetteer.

Newspapers Foreign newspapers and books are readily available in bookshops and kiosks in all main cities and many resort hotels. They are rather expensive.

Opening Times There are considerable local variations, but the following are guidelines for main cities.

Shops: Denmark Mon.–Thurs. 0900–1730, Fri. 0900–1900/2000, Sat. 0900–1200/1400. **Finland** Tues.–Thurs. 0830/0900–1700/1730, Mon. and Fri. 0830/0900–2000, Sat. 0830/0900–1300/1400. Longer hours in subway shopping centre by Helsinki Railway Station. **Iceland** Mon.–Fri. 0900–1800, Sat. 0900–1200 (some shops close Sat. in summer). **Norway** Mon.–Fri. 0900–1600/1700, Sat. 0900–1300/1400. Some shops open longer hours one day a week; those at Grønland subway, Oslo, open to 2230. **Sweden** Mon.–Fri. 0900/0930–1700/1800, Sat. 0900–1300/1600. Some department stores open to 2000/2200 once or twice weekly.

Photography The only restrictions are clearly marked: in some museums, near military installations or anywhere within some distance of the Soviet border. Some Same (Lapp) people in the far north prefer not to be photographed; it is courteous to ask them.

Police Throughout the area, the police uniform is dark blue or black, with light blue shirt and dark overcoat in winter. Swedish road patrols often wear green overalls. Winter headgear in Finland, Norway and Sweden is a fur hat. Police are usually friendly and helpful.

Postal Services (see also Telephones, below) Post boxes, usually attached to a wall, are red in Denmark, Iceland and Norway, and yellow in Finland and Sweden. Postage stamps are readily available from hotels, kiosks, tobacconists and some bookshops as well as post offices. Normal post office opening hours are given below, but these will be longer at main offices in the cities. **Denmark** Mon.–Fri. 0900/1000–1700/1730, Sat. 0900–1200; **Finland** Mon.–Fri. 0900–

1700, Sat. closed (except main post office); **Iceland** Mon.–Fri. 0800/0900–1700, Sat. 0900–1200; **Norway** Mon.–Fri. 0800–1700/1730 (summer 1630), Sat. 0900–1200; **Sweden** Mon.–Fri. 0800/0900–1800, Sat. 0800/0900–1300 (some branches closed Sats. in July).

Public Holidays The following are public holidays throughout the area: 1 Jan., Good Friday, Easter Monday, 1 May (except Denmark), Ascension Day, Whit Monday, 25 and 26 Dec. Additional ones are: **Denmark** Maundy Thurs. (day before Good Friday), Day of Prayer (fourth Fri. after Good Friday); **Finland** Epiphany (Sat. nearest 6 Jan.), Midsummer Day (Sat. nearest 24 June), All Saints Day (Sat. at end Oct. or early Nov.), 6 Dec. (Independence Day); **Iceland** Maundy Thurs. (day before Good Friday), 22 April (first day of summer), August Bank Holiday (first Mon. in Aug.); **Norway** Maundy Thurs. (day before Good Friday), 17 May (Constitution Day); **Sweden** 6 Jan. (Epiphany), Midsummer Day (Sat. nearest 24 June), All Saints Day (Sat. at end Oct. or early Nov.). On these days banks, offices and most shops are closed.

Shopping (see also Opening Times, above) Scandinavia is famous for design and quality. Items in glass, ceramics, wood, stainless steel and also textiles are of a high standard. In addition, **Denmark** is particularly noted for amber and handmade pipes; **Finland** for fashion goods in marvellous colours; **Iceland** for beautiful knitwear in natural wool colours, and interesting lavaware; **Norway** for pewter, silver, enamelware, distinctive knitwear; **Sweden** for cut glass and household gadgets.

Traditional crafts and designs drawn from folk cultures are kept very much alive and many regional handicrafts organizations ensure high quality. There is also attractive jewellery, often incorporating semi-precious stones, extracted, cut and polished in remoter areas of the far north. Many museums sell well-made replicas of ancient artistry. Beautiful furs are also good, if more expensive, buys. At the other end of the scale is an enormous variety of candles which all Scandinavians put to good decorative use. Some tasty food and drink items are mentioned in the section Food and Drink.

A high sales tax (*moms* in Denmark, Norway and Sweden) is imposed and can be avoided (except in Iceland) especially by having your purchases sent to your home address or, in some cases, direct to the airport or ship (notably in Finland and Sweden, or ship only in Norway), providing the value is above a substantial minimum and the goods purchased from shops offering this facility. The regulations for taking goods with you can, however, be complicated and should be checked locally.

Telephones Public telephone boxes are well distributed in town streets. Except for Denmark, you will not find them in post offices but in special Telegraph offices (marked *Tele* or, in Finland, *Lennätin*). The procedure is to lift the receiver, insert the money and dial; if you are not connected, the money is returned, except in Denmark where it is therefore advisable to start with the lowest coins. 'Charges for calls from hotels can be quite expensive. Except in a few remote areas, there is long-distance direct automatic dialling throughout, and also to Britain and North America, though this is not always possible from public boxes. When checking a number in the telephone directory, remember that names beginning with Scandinavian letters such as Ä, Å, Ö, Ø come at the end of the alphabet. In Iceland, entries are under Christian names.

Time Differential Iceland is on Greenwich Mean Time; Denmark, Norway and Sweden are 1 hour ahead; Finland 2 hours ahead. As in most countries in Europe all, except Iceland, apply 'summer time' which means from late Mar. to late Sept. time is 2–3 hours later than GMT. Since this period coincides within a month of 'daylight saving time' in Britain (late Mar.–late Oct.) and the United States (late Apr.–late Oct.), the time differential remains the same for most of the year: in **Finland** is 2 hours ahead of British time, 7 hours behind US Eastern Time; **Denmark, Norway** and **Sweden** are 1 hour ahead of British time, 6 hours behind US Eastern Time; **Iceland** is 1 hour behind British time in summer, on the same time in winter, and 4 hours behind US Eastern Time in summer, 5 hours in winter.

Tipping A service charge is included in hotel and restaurant bills throughout the area and extra tipping is not as prevalent as in many other parts of the world. (In Iceland there is no tipping at all.)

Good service in a restaurant is usually acknowledged by sums ranging from a few low denomination coins to, say, 10 per cent depending on the standard of restaurant. It is also usual practice to leave your coat in the cloakroom for which there is a fixed charge, or to tip the doorman a similar sum. Taxi drivers and hairdressers do not expect tips, except in Sweden where 10–15 per cent is considered normal. Railway porters, if you can find them, operate on fixed charges.

Toilets Standards in hotels, restaurants,

department stores are generally very high, but those of other public toilets do vary and are not always up to Scandinavia's usual high standard. In some places, especially in rural areas, you may need to ask for the key. The sexes are often indicated by the small figure of a man or woman. Otherwise the words to look out for are: **Denmark** *herrer, damer*; **Finland** 'H' or *miehille*, 'D' or *naisille*; **Iceland** *karlar, konur*; **Norway** *herrer, damer*; **Sweden** *herrar, damer*.

USEFUL ADDRESSES

(tel. nos in brackets)

Scandinavian Tourist Offices: UK Danish Tourist Board, Sceptre House, 169/173 Regent St., London W1R 8PY (01 734 2637); Finnish Tourist Board, 66 Haymarket, London SW1 4RF (01 839 4048); Iceland Tourist Information Bureau, 73 Grosvenor St., London W1X 9DD (01 493 4619); Norwegian Tourist Board, 20 Pall Mall, London SW1Y 5NE (01 839 6255); Swedish National Tourist Office, 3 Cork St., London W1X 1HA (01 437 5816). **USA** All countries: 75 Rockefeller Plaza, New York, NY10019 (212 582 2802). **Canada** Danish National Tourist Office, 151 Bloor St. West, 8th floor, Toronto M5S 1S4, Ontario (416 960 3305).

British Consulates: Denmark Kastelsvej 36–40, 2100 Copenhagen Ø (01 264600), also in Åbenra, Ålborg, Århus, Esbjerg, Fredericia, Odense; **Finland** Uudenmaankatu 16–20, 00120 Helsinki 12 (90 12574), also Oulu, Pori, Tampere, Turku, Vaasa; **Iceland** Laugavegur 49, Reykjavik (15883/4), also Akureyri, Isafjördur; **Norway** Thomas Heftyesgate 8, Oslo 2 (02 563890/7), also Ålesund, Bergen, Haugesund, Kristiansund (N), Narvik, Stavanger, Tromsø, Trondheim; **Sweden** Skarpögatan 6–8, 11527 Stockholm (08 670140), also Gothenburg, Malmö.

US Embassies: Denmark Dag Hammarskjölds Allé 24, 2100 Copenhagen Ø (01 423144); **Finland** I. Puistotie 14A, 00140 Helsinki 14 (90 171931); **Iceland** Laugavegur 21, Reykjavík (29100); **Norway** Drammensveien 18, Oslo (02 566880); **Sweden** Strandvägen 101, 11527 Stockholm (08 630520).

Canadian Embassies: Denmark Prinsesse Maries Allé 2, 1908 Copenhagen V (01 313306); **Finland** Pohjoisesplanadi 25B, 00100 Helsinki 10 (90 171141); **Norway** Oscars gate 20, Oslo (02 466955); **Sweden** Tegelbacken 4, 10323 Stockholm (08 237920).

Air Services   Air UK, Norwich

Airport, Norwich, Norfolk NR6 6ER (01 551 4988); British Airways, West London Terminal, Cromwell Rd, London SW7 (01 370 5411); Dan-Air, Lennig House, Masons Ave, Croydon, Surrey (01 680 1011); Finnair, 56 Haymarket, London SW1 (01 930 3941); Icelandair, 73 Grosvenor St., London W1X 9DD (01 680 4619); Northwest Orient, Pegasus House, Sackville St., London W1X 1DB (01 439 0171); Scandinavian Airlines (SAS), 52–3 Conduit St., London W1 (01 734 4020).

Shipping services Baltic Shipping Co., 24–26 Baltic St., London EC1Y 0TB (01 253 3456); DFDS Danish Seaways, DFDS Prins Ferries and DFDS Tor Line, Latham House, 16 Minories, London EC3N 1AN (01 481 3211); Faroese Coastal Service (same address as Regent Holidays under Specialist UK Tour Operators, below); Sealink, PO Box 29, London SW1V 1JX (01 834 8122/2345); Townsend Thoresen, 9–13 St Andrew St., London EC4A 2AE (01 583 9330).

Motoring Organizations Automobile Association, Fanum House, Basingstoke, Hants. RG21 2EA (0256 20123); Royal Automobile Club, RAC House, Lansdowne Rd, Croydon CR0 2JA (01 686 2525); Forenede Danske Motorejere (FDM), Blegdamsvej 124, 2100 Copenhagen Ø (01 382112); Autoliitto (Automobile and Touring Club of Finland), Kansakoulukatu 10, 00100 Helsinki 10 (90 6940022); Norges Automobil-Forbund (NAF), Storgate 2, Oslo (02 337080); Kongelig Norsk Automobilklub (KNA), Parkveien 68, Oslo 2 (02 562690); Motormännens Riksförbund (M), Sturegatan 32, 10240 Stockholm (08 670580); Kungliga Automobilklubben (KAK), Wahrendorffsgatan 1, 10320 Stockholm (08 238800).

Some Specialist UK Tour Operators Countrywide Holiday Association (CHA), Birch Heys, Cromwell Range, Manchester M14 6HU (061 2242887); DFDS Danish Seaways, Latham House, 16 Minories, London EC3N 1AN (01 481 3211); Finlandia Travel Agency, 49 Whitcomb St., London WC2H 7OH (01 839 4741); Norway Only, Norway House, 126 Sunbridge Rd, Bradford, West Yorkshire BD1 2SX (0274 35611); Norwegian State Railways, 21–24 Cockspur St., London SW1Y 5DA (01 930 6666); Fred Olsen Travel, 11 Conduit St., London W1R 0LS (01 491 3760); Dick Phillips, Whitehall House, Nenthead, Alston, Cumbria CA9 3PS (04983 440); Ramblers Holidays, 13 Longcroft House, Fretherne Rd, Welwyn Garden City, Herts. AL8 6PQ (07073 31133); E. Raymond & Co., 25 Prudential

Buildings, 36 Dale St., Liverpool L2 5SW (051 236 2960); Regent Holidays, Regent House, Regent St., Shanklin, Isle of Wight PO37 7AE (098386 4212); Scantours, 8 Spring Gdns, London SW1 (01 839 2927); Swedish State Railways, as for Norwegian State Railways; Tor Holidays, Anzani House, Trinity Ave, Felixstowe, Suffolk IP11 8XE (03942 73131); Twickenham Travel, 84 Hampton Rd, Twickenham, Middlesex TW2 5QS (01 898 8221); YHA Travel, 14 Southampton St., London WC2E 7HY (01 836 8541).

Some Specialist Addresses in Scandinavia Dantourist, Hulgade 21, 5700 Svendborg, Denmark; Norwegian Mountain Touring Association (DNT), Stortingsgt. 28, Oslo 1, Norway; Swedish Touring Club (STF), Box 7615, 10394 Stockholm, Sweden.

LANGUAGE

With the exception of Finnish, the Scandinavian languages belong to one of three divisions of the Germanic branch of Indo-European languages. Despite the quite marked differences in their languages, Danes, Norwegians and Swedes can understand each other with relative ease. In Norway, the situation is slightly complicated by the fact that, until 1905, when it seceded from Sweden, the official language was Danish and the current majority language, called *riksmål* Norwegian (or 'book Norwegian'), is substantially influenced by Danish. About 100 years ago there began a strong movement to revive the older Norwegian dialects, now called *landsmål* (or 'new Norwegian') and both are taught in schools and used in government service. *Riksmål* Norwegian still predominates, however, except in the rural areas of western Norway.

In the case of Iceland, much greater isolation has resulted in a language that is virtually unchanged from the Norse of medieval times, and Icelanders can read their ancient sagas without any problems; you might compare this to a modern English-speaking student being able to read Chaucer with ease. They have also retained the old system of patronymics. Thus Jón Sigurdsson is Jón, the son of Sigurd; his son Sveinn becomes Sveinn Jónsson and his daughter Helga, Helga Jónsdóttir. And so on. Women do not change their names when they marry. So, if you want to trace anyone through the telephone directory, you look for them under their Christian name. There is a strong movement to protect the Icelandic language from the introduction of foreign words.

Swedish is also the second official language of Finland where it is the mother tongue of a minority of about 6 per cent. The Finnish language itself belongs to the Finno-Ugrian group (together, for example, with Estonian and Hungarian) and, with its 14 grammatical cases, appears very difficult, though it is extremely logical and, like the Scandinavian languages, phonetic. Until the national revival movement of the 19th century, Finnish was largely the language of the less privileged. It was the publication of such epic works as *Kalevala* (p. 11) that helped Finns to a new awareness of their cultural heritage.

The alphabet includes a few extra letters: ä (Finnish and Swedish), å (Danish and Swedish), ö (Finnish, Icelandic and Swedish), ø (Danish and Norwegian). Note that these come at the end of the alphabet, an important point to remember when referring to an index or directory. Icelandic also retains two consonants from ancient Norse; ð (similar to *d*) and þ (*th* as in thin). Since the pronunciation of certain combinations of letters (such as *sk* before some vowels or *g* at the end of words) varies from one country to another, it is a good idea to learn the basics if only to pronounce place names correctly when seeking directions.

English is very widely taught and spoken throughout Scandinavia, though rather less generally in Finland, especially among the older generation. On the whole, there are few areas of the non-English speaking world where you are less likely to meet language problems.

DENMARK

Denmark's area of approximately 43,000 sq km/16,600 sq mi is roughly twice the size of Wales and carries a population of about five million. Apart from Jutland, it consists of nearly 500 islands of which 100 are inhabited, giving a total coastline of 7300 km/4500 mi. Though it lacks the high scenic drama of its northern neighbours, its countryside is fair and fertile, and the relaxed Danes have an easy-going friendliness that is not quite so manifest in their fellow Scandinavians.

Denmark's two highest points (both 170 m/557 ft) are in east Jutland. By far the most predominant features of its landscapes are the undulating, well-husbanded farmlands punctuated by woods and the huddle of pretty villages or farm complexes, often of considerable age. There is something timeless and relaxing about these tidy landscapes, though the wind of change is in evidence

as reduced dairy herds lead to increasing arable production and rosy pigs disappear into the warm sheds of factory farming. It remains, however, an ideal and well-organized country for the farmhouse holiday with its very special family appeal; ideal, too, for motorists and cyclists for whom there are excellent facilities. Note that the distances given in the gazetteer apply to road distances and time should be allowed for ferry crossings where appropriate.

There is much to see: rich collections dating back to prehistory, numerous traces from Viking times, many castles and monasteries reflecting the prosperity of the Middle Ages when the great forests were cleared. Christianity was introduced by the monk Ansgar (826–865) and the village church became a major feature of rural Denmark along with the half-timbered farms and inns. It was the monks who taught the people to burn clay, accounting for the predominance of brick as a building material throughout the country. Later came the castles, manors and parks reflecting and adapting the Renaissance styles especially from Holland. Excellent free booklets on the village church and on castles and manor houses are available from the Danish Tourist Board.

Denmark's other great natural feature is the complexity of its coastlines, providing splendid sheltered waters for boating, bathing, fishing and other water sports. Among the stirring sights of the Danish summer is the fluttering of a myriad colourful sails during the round-Funen and (especially) round-Sealand regattas which attract not only the experts but large-scale family participation. A terrestrial equivalent are the marches or organized walks (p.23) in which many hundreds take part.

Culturally there is plenty doing from jazz and medieval jousting to street theatre and the Royal Danish Ballet. Denmark's pleasure gardens – Copenhagen's Tivoli is simply the largest and most sophisticated – typify the Danish talent for catering for all tastes and all ages in the same place at the same time.

JUTLAND, FUNEN LANGELAND, ÆRØ

JUTLAND

Jutland is the only part of Denmark attached to the continent of Europe, a fact that has caused it many problems throughout its history. Its southern approach across the narrow neck of flat lands shared with Germany's Schleswig Holstein has always been vulnerable and the border frequently disputed. Dutch and German architectural influences are very apparent in the little towns of south Jutland.

As early as the 9th century, a defensive system of earthworks called Danevirke (now in Germany) was begun by King Godfred to protect his lands from Charlemagne. The most recent contest over this border was the Danish–Prussian War which resulted in much of south Jutland being ceded to Prussia in 1864 (part of it was re-united with Denmark in 1920). These territorial losses included Jutland's most fertile land. Much of the rest of the peninsula consisted of unproductive bog and heath. So serious was this for the country's economy that the Heath Institute was created to do battle with the moorland. The reclamation was arduous toil which eventually earned the cultivators a memorial park near Viborg, but it was very effective: about 900,000 hectares or 2¼ million acres (90 per cent) of the moorland was reclaimed, and it is now the turn of the moorland to be protected by the same Institute.

A curious phenomenon of the Jutland bog is its preservative properties; hence the astonishing number of 'bog people' – corpses in such remarkable condition that after 2000 years they retain, in some cases, a growth of beard, a profusion of hair and even the discernible remains of their last meal. Notable examples are in Silkeborg and Århus. Iron Age (eg Århus) and Viking finds (eg Lindholm Høje, Jelling) are numerous. Even more numerous are the stone churches and beautiful half-timbered buildings from medieval times onwards, collected into notable open-air museums at Hjerl Hede and Århus, but also to be seen in towns and villages all over the peninsula.

The much-fragmented west coast is another attraction, with its big lagoonlike fjords, and the great waterway complex of Limfjord that links the North Sea with the Kattegat. Some of the beaches are uninterrupted for miles, often firm enough to be driven on, and backed by rolling sand dunes. Most of Denmark's amber is washed up on these beaches, especially after autumn storms. The bird life is varied, with several nature reserves (eg Tipperne). Many rivers, flowing in all directions from the heathery hills, offer good fishing, and one of them, the Gudenå, winding northwards to Randers through the central lake district, provides an idyllic, though sometimes over-crowded, canoeing route.

Ålborg F6

(pop. 155,000) Denmark's fourth largest town faces industrial **Nørresundby** to which it is linked by bridges and a tunnel across Limfjord. The centre of the town has great charm with narrow lanes and houses from the 15th–19th centuries, notably Aalborghus (1539; once the building of the royal exchequer), Jorgen Olufsen's House (1616), and Jens Bang's impressive, if ostentatious, 5-story Stone House (1624) next to the Old Town Hall (1762). The tourist office, opposite the last-named, makes a good starting point for exploring on foot and has excellent leaflets to direct your footsteps. Nearby, the cathedral (Budolfidomkirke) has been rebuilt and expanded over 800 years; much of it, including the spire, is Baroque. Helligåndsklostret (1431), a monastery sheltering a home for the elderly, is beautifully preserved. The ultramodern North Jutland Museum of Art (Aalto and Baruël) has very fine Danish and foreign collections, and the Historical Museum includes some excellent glass and silver. There is also a large, well-arranged zoo and Tivoliland pleasure gardens with varied entertainment. This is, indeed, a lively cosmopolitan town with a wide choice of restaurants, wine bars, discos and night clubs.

In the east part of town is 12th-century Nørre Tranders Church (stone carvings, frescoes). To the north overlooking the industrial landscapes of Nørresundby is **Lindholm Høje**, a remarkable Iron Age and Viking cemetery in which 682 graves are scattered about a hillside, many of their stone settings in distinctive boat shapes. Here, too, is a field bearing the furrows and plough marks of 1000 years ago. The Skagerrak coast, a short drive north west of Ålborg, is a huge expanse of beach fringed with extensive sand dunes; the beach is so firm that you can drive along it for miles, *eg* from **Blokhus** to **Løkken**. A little north east of Blokhus is **Fårup Sommerland**, a family playground of considerable size; the entrance fee covers the use of all kinds of sporting facilities. *Esbjerg 228km/141mi.*

Århus   I7
(pop. 250,000) Founded in Viking times, this is Denmark's second largest city. After a period of stagnation following the Reformation, it rose to become a major trading centre and industrial city with a busy harbour. There are ferry connections with Kalundborg on Sealand. The oldest church is the Church of our Lady (from 1100) under whose choir an 11th-century crypt church was discovered in recent years. The upper part of the interior is Gothic with late medieval frescoes. The cathedral is in the late Gothic style of the 15th century, though founded in the 13th. It has the longest nave and biggest organ in Denmark, medieval choir stalls, a fine altarpiece (1479), and many wall paintings.

Occupying part of the Botanical Garden is an outstanding open-air museum, Den gamle By (Old Town), a collection of 60 half-timbered town houses and shops from different parts of Denmark dating from 1600–1860. The modern Town Hall has a façade in Greenland marble.

On the north side of town, Århus University is set in rolling parkland. On the south side is the Tivoli-Friheden amusement park and, beyond it, the beautiful Memorial Park, with a monument to World War I, set in beech woods and opening out on to the bay. Nearby, the park of the Queen's summer residence, Marselisborg, with beautiful rose gardens, is open to the public when she is not in residence. Also south of town, in the manor house of Moesgård is an exceptionally fine Museum of Prehistory with collections from the Iron Age (mummified body of Grauballe Man, about 1600 years old) and Viking Age runic stones. A 'prehistoric track' leads from here past sundry original and reconstructed prehistoric structures (dolmens, barrows, houses). *Esbjerg 152km/94mi.*

Ebeltoft   I8
(pop. 3000) The old core of the town is a truly picture-postcard place of cobbled streets lined with half-timbered houses, very well preserved and many from the 16th–18th centuries, including some excellent inns and eating places. A town crier does his rounds every summer evening. This is the main town of the Mols region, characterized by the wooded and heath-covered Mols hills which offer good walking. From the ferry harbour south of town there are frequent connections with Sjaellands Odde on Sealand. *Esbjerg 209km/129mi.*

Esbjerg   L3
(pop. 72,000) For many visitors busy Esbjerg provides their first glimpse of Denmark, yet not much more than 100 years ago there was little here but a handful of farms. Esbjerg grew with the development of the harbour from 1868, the arrival of the railway, shipping links with the UK and the fishing fleets which today make it Denmark's largest fishing port. The lively goings-on in the Fish Auction Hall (from 0700) are among Esbjerg's attractions. It also has a particularly well-equipped Fishery and Maritime Museum. In 20 minutes by ferry you can reach the holiday island of **Fanø** (pop. 3000; 55sq km/21sq mi) with its huge and popular expanses of beach on which it is possible to drive for many miles. In its heyday of the 18th–19th centuries, Fanø had a sizeable fleet of sailing ships many of whose skippers lived in the delightful community of **Sønderho** in the south of the island. A lot of the old houses are protected and the church is notable for its ship models. **Nordby**, where the ferry lands, is the biggest centre (Fanø Museum). The island has innumerable holiday homes and is packed in summer. *Copenhagen 278km/172mi.*

Frederikshavn   D8
(pop. 35,000) This is a major port, fishing and industrial centre, with regular sea connections to Larvik and Oslo in Norway, Gothenburg in Sweden, and the Danish island of **Laesø** which is an unspoilt haven of meadows, moor and sand dunes, with several pretty churches and seaweed-thatched farms. Frederikshavn has some 17th-century houses and the 18th-century manor house, Bangsbo, is a museum with excellent collections from the Stone Age to World War II. *Esbjerg 290km/180mi.*

Grenå   H8
(pop. 15,600) This manufacturing town on the coast of the peninsula of Djursland is mainly known for its modern harbour from which there are car-ferry links with Hundested in Sealand, Helsingborg and Varberg in Sweden, and the islet of Anholt. The Djursland countryside is charming and dotted with pretty villages and manor houses. **Anholt** covers 22sq km/8½sq mi and has 160 inhabitants. It is a haven for escapists in search of peace.

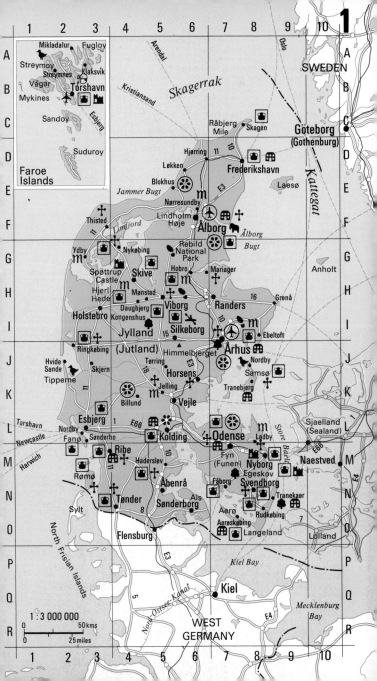

There are mini desertlike stretches of drifting sand, stony plains and dunes, and you can cycle or walk all round the island along the beach. *Esbjerg 214km/132mi.*

Haderslev   M5
(pop. 30,000) The town sprawls between the head of Haderslev fjord and a lake. It is an ancient market · town, with 16th-century houses featuring Dutch-style bay windows, and dominated by its red-brick medieval cathedral. The archaeological collection in the regional museum is particularly fine and includes a copy of the Skrydstrup Girl's dress from about 1300 BC. Old half-timbered farms and other buildings may be seen in the open-air section of the museum. *Esbjerg 80km/50mi.*

Horsens   K6
(pop. 45,000) This town on Horsens fjord was a prosperous trading centre in the 18th century, from which time a number of merchants' houses of substance survive. It had developed earlier round its medieval abbey whose church has rich interiors (15th-century carvings). Today there is some industry. *Esbjerg 110km/68mi.*

Kolding   L5
(pop. 55,000) Today an industrial town, Kolding began as a medieval fortress, then abbey and trading centre. For centuries, Koldinghus (13th century, but reconstructed after fire), was a royal residence; now it houses a museum and fine library. The Geographical Gardens are notable; plants from all over the world include Northern Europe's biggest bamboo grove and 10,000 roses. *Esbjerg 72km/44mi.*

Mariager   H6
(pop. 2000) This is a charming little market town on a fjord of the same name; it developed round 15th-century St Bridget Abbey. There is a number of old churches in the surroundings (**Dalbyneder, Udbyneder** and **Visborg**), but of particular interest is the Viking Age encampment of **Fyrkat** (10km/6mi W) near the small industrial town of **Hobro** (Viking Museum). *Esbjerg 202km/125mi.*

Nykøbing   G4
(pop. 9000) The town is the principal community on the island of Mors in Limfjord (bridge and ferry connections). Its heyday was in the 15th–17th centuries, the great period of the herring fishery. Today it is a main centre of the oyster industry for which Limfjord is well known. The 14th-century abbey round which the town developed is now a historical museum. *Esbjerg 164km/102mi.*

Rebild National Park   G6
In 1912, Danish-Americans purchased this natural amphitheatre in the heathery hills of north Jutland and presented it to the Danish nation. The Lincoln Log Cabin was built to house an Emigrant Museum. The celebrations held here each 4 July are the biggest anywhere in or out of the United States. The surrounding region of Rold Forest and the Rebild Hills is very beautiful and includes Denmark's largest woodland area. It is a fine area for walking. *Esbjerg 210km/130mi.*

Ribe   M3
(pop. 8250) This is one of the oldest and prettiest towns in Scandinavia, and has been an episcopal seat since 948. Its fine five-aisled cathedral was founded in the 12th century on the highest point, though today the surrounding houses, built over the centuries on successive layers of rubble, stand a little above it. There are over 100 protected houses from the 16th–18th centuries and enormous care is taken to ensure that repairs and restorations maintain the original styles. The local tourist association plays a vital part in what is an unusually enlightened programme of urban conservation, by which private owners may obtain interest-free loans provided their restored building is properly maintained.

A stroll through the narrow streets with their red-brick, half-timbered or colour-washed houses is very rewarding. Buildings of special note include the Cathedral School (Denmark's oldest), the Town Hall (1528), St Catharine's Church and the delightful convent buildings (1228; now a charitable foundation), and Quedens Gaard (museum in a merchant's four-winged house). Every summer evening the nightwatchman does his colourful rounds. In summer you can take a river boat trip from Skibbroen, the old harbour, through unspoilt marshlands to the sea. To the south west, the island of **Rømø** (old church, regional museum) is reached by a 10km/6mi causeway; it is a place of heath, marsh, extensive sand dunes and great beaches. *Esbjerg 30km/18mi.*

Ringkøbing   J2
(pop. 6500) This charming little west-coast town was an important fishing and cattle-trading centre in the 16th–17th centuries, and its narrow streets and lovely old houses echo those times. The brick church is late medieval, and the museum includes a Greenland depart-

Århus

Ribe

Lacemaking, Tønder

ment. To the south are the great expanses of the lagoonlike Ringkøbing fjord, separated from the North Sea by the 40km/25mi-long isthmus of Holmslands Klit with its sand dunes, beaches and lively fishing port of **Hvide Sande**. In the south of the fjord is the chunky peninsula of **Tipperne** on which there is one of Scandinavia's top bird sanctuaries (open limited hours without a permit on Sundays). *Esbjerg 80km/50mi.*

Samsø   K8

(pop. 4900) This shoe-shaped island lies about halfway between central Jutland and Funen and is linked to both by ferry. Its 114sq km/44sq mi are quite unspoilt – plenty of beaches, rolling dunes and meadowland, and interesting bird life. In the north, **Nordby** is a pretty village of half-timbered farms. In the south is **Brattingsborg**, a 19th-century manor house with English garden. Roughly central, **Tranebjerg** (pop. 660) is the island's biggest community with a museum farm (Samsø Museumsgård) and 14th-century church.

Silkeborg   I5

(pop. 46,500) In the heart of the central

Jutland lake district, Silkeborg is a pleasant small lakeside town. Its Provincial Museum is a gem and contains two of Scandinavia's greatest curiosities: Tollund Man and Elling Woman, discovered in a remarkable state of preservation in nearby bogs. Both died over 2000 years ago by hanging, possibly as offerings to a god. Tollund Man is the better preserved, his lined face in gentle repose with a day or so's growth of stubble. Elling Woman has little face but a fine crop of plaited hair. From Silkeborg there are lake tours by paddle steamer and other boats to the foot of **Himmelbjerget**, Denmark's second highest hill (147m/482ft). The town also lies about halfway along a popular canoeing route, an idyllic, if at times crowded, 160km/100mi stretch of river and lake waters from **Tørring** to **Randers**, which can be joined at Silkeborg. *Esbjerg 139km/86mi.*

Skagen   C8

(pop. 13,000) This is a delightful town near the tip of Jutland. About 75 per cent of its economy is based on fishing, and the comings and goings of its fishing fleets, its fish auctions and the bustle of activity in the harbour are among its great attractions. Rows of little red-painted store-houses from the turn of the century line the quaysides and add to the visual appeal. The way of life of the old days is well preserved in the open-air museum of Skagens Fortidsminder. Skagen became well known throughout northern Europe because of the artists who flocked here in the late 19th and early 20th centuries, attracted by the pure light, the prettiness of the place and the windswept heaths and sand dunes. Many of their works may be seen in the Skagen Museum or in the Brøndum Hotel. Artists include Michael and Anna Ancher, P.S. Kroyer and the Norwegian Christian Krogh. The Anchers' house is also a museum. Painting holidays are arranged by the tourist office each summer.

Grenen, the windswept northernmost point of Jutland, is only 5km/3mi away, with yet another art museum (modern). Here, where the waters of the Skagerrak and Kattegat meet and crash against the long beaches, are several generations of lighthouse. One, near town, is a re-construction of a 16th-century bascule, or seesaw, light. West of town, the tower of a buried church rises out of the sand. **Rå-bjerg Mile**, a few miles south west, is an extraordinary expanse of high sand dunes. From nearby **Kandestederne** you can drive along the beach for several miles to **Skiveren**. *Esbjerg 337 km/209mi.*

Skive   H4

(pop. 27,000) This small industrial town is on Skive fjord, one of the southern ramifications of the complex Limfjord system. Skive Museum's archaeological collections include Denmark's biggest amber find and an interesting Greenland collection. But the town's main attraction is as a launching point for several places of interest in the Limfjord countryside. **Hjerl Hede** (20km/12mi SW) is an ex-ceptionally fine and still expanding open-air museum set in extensive protected forest and moorland by Lake Flynndersø. It consists of about 40 buildings from different parts of the country, among them Denmark's oldest farm, a church, school, workshops, *etc*. There is also a Stone Age settlement in which the daily life of 5000 years ago is re-created every July. **Spøttrup Castle** (19km/11mi NW of Skive) is a splendidly restored medieval castle rising out of encircling double moats. *Esbjerg 143km/88mi.*

Thisted   F3

(pop. 13,000) In a splendid situation on the shores of Limfjord, this small indus-trial town has a Renaissance church. The surroundings have yielded many prehis-toric sites, notably **Ydby Skjold**, a collec-tion of 32 Bronze Age burial mounds near Ydby to the south west. The nearby heath-fringed Skagerrak coast has glo-rious beaches and from Hanstholm, a few miles north, there are sea links to the Faroes, Bergen and Kristiansand. *Esbjerg 182km/113mi.*

Tønder   N4

(pop. 7400) This pretty town, in the centre of a cattle-breeding area near the border with Germany, has changed hands many times in its history. It has fine houses from the 17th and 18th centuries and a good regional museum illustrating traditional crafts of the area (lace, silver, *etc*). The church (1592) has a rich interior. *Esbjerg 77km/48mi.*

Vejle   K5

(pop. 49,000) The town, which developed round the head of Vejle fjord, is mainly interesting for its surroundings of wooded slopes characteristic of east Jutland. There are summer boat trips on the fjord and a veteran railway runs through the pretty Grejs valley. At **Jelling** (11km/7mi W) are the 10th-century royal burial mounds and runic stones associated with King Gorm the Old and his Queen Thyra. One of the runic stones in the churchyard bears perhaps Scandinavia's oldest rep-resentation of Christ, surrounded by Viking Age animal decoration. It is dedi-cated to Gorm by his son Harald Bluetooth 'who conquered Denmark and Norway and made his people Christian'. The church has Denmark's oldest, but restored, frescoes (12th century).

At **Billund** (28km/17mi W of Vejle) is the very different attraction of Legoland, a miniature world created out of 15 million of the famous interlocking plastic com-ponents, from Dutch canal landscapes to temples of the Far East. Another popular exhibit is Titania's Palace, originally built by Sir Nevile Wilkinson for his daughter (completed 1922) and quite astonishing in its detail and workmanship. An excellent Doll Museum, a traffic school, Wild West town and pony riding are among other features which make this one of Scandinavia's top family attractions. *Esbjerg 83km/51mi.*

Viborg   H5

(pop. 28,000) For about 600 years, until the early 17th century, this ancient town was Jutland's capital. It lies in the central lake district amid rolling farmland. The granite cathedral was built about 100 years ago on the site of a series of earlier churches; its 19th-century starkness was alleviated early this century by the frescoes of Joakim Skovgaard and his team, who created a kind of pictorial Bible with over 50 scenes. Søndre Sogns Church has been largely restored to its original medieval condition, retaining later valuable additions such as the 18th-century pews embellished with more than 200 paintings. Many of the old red-brick houses of the town centre from the 16th century onwards are being restored; the general effect is charming and well worth some footwork.

At **Kongenshus**, in the countryside to the south west, is a memorial park and a museum to the heath cultivators who transformed their unproductive land-scapes; here you can see how much of Jutland looked only 100 years ago. This can be combined with a visit to the huge lime pits near **Mønsted** (35km/21mi of galleries) and **Daugbjerg** (probably in use since Viking times), west of Viborg. Viborg is also at the northern end of the old Military Road (*Haervej*), a historic track and now a walking and cycling route which follows the Jutland watershed south to the German border. There is an organized 2-day walk along it in late June. *Esbjerg 155km/96mi.*

FUNEN LANGELAND AERØ

With justification Funen is referred to as 'the garden of Denmark'. Its neatness has a prosperous look drawn from the rich soils and their high yields. Stone walls or hedges add orderliness to the scene, while woods contribute their deeper green flourish. Odense is the main city, made famous by its renowned son Hans Christian Andersen. South Funen and the islands of Aerø and Langeland have the particular charm of areas lying off main through routes.

Aerøskøbing   O7
(pop. 1300) This is the principal com-munity on the island of Aerø, reached by ferry from Svendborg or Fåborg on Funen, and from Monmark, south Jutland. For 500 years the island formed part of Schleswig whose influence is marked in the architectural styles. The island is a delightful rural backwater and Aerøskøbing itself is near-perfect, with nothing to jar the harmony of its tiny streets and half-timbered houses from the

15th–19th centuries. One of them, the Bailiff's House, contains the Aerø Museum and Old Pharmacy. The post office (1749) is Denmark's oldest. There is also a substantial bottle ship collection.

Egeskov   M7
In the heart of the Funen countryside, this is one of Denmark's worthiest castles and, indeed, one of Europe's best-preserved island forts. It was built (1524–54) on a foundation of oak pillars wedged into the bottom of a small lake, so that it rises literally out of the water (access by bridge). With its pink stonework it is a most pleasing sight and its sur-rounding park is famous for Renaissance, Baroque and modern landscaping, a maze of 200-year-old hedges and a magnificent fuchsia garden. Part of the estate is an ancient barn now containing the Egeskov Veteran Museum of aircraft, cars and other vehicles. *Esbjerg 162km/101mi.*

Fåborg   N7
(pop. 6500) This picturesque old town has ferry connections with Als, south Jutland, the island of Aerø and some smaller islands, and Gelting in north Germany. It has many old houses, and a well-preserved west gate, one of few town gates surviving in Denmark. Den gamle Gård museum has interesting local collec-tions, and Fåborg Museum is devoted to the works of Funen painters. The bell tower is from 1475. *Esbjerg 160km/100mi.*

Nyborg   M8
(pop. 14,300) In medieval times, this was the heavily fortified administrative hub of Denmark, seat of parliament and scene of the signing of the country's oldest consti-tution in 1282. Its 12th-century castle, restored earlier this century, can be vis-ited. From its commanding position on the coast, this splendid pile guarded the Great Belt between Funen and Sealand, though much of its grandeur was lost when King Frederick IV had bricks quar-ried from its massive walls to build his palace in Odense. Nyborg Museum is in an attractive 17th-century merchant's half-timbered house. From the nearby harbour of Knudshoved there are regular ferry crossings over the Great Belt to Halsskovhavn on Sealand. *Esbjerg 167km/104mi.*

Odense   L7
(pop. 170,000) Odense is Denmark's third biggest city, linked by a 7km/4mi canal to the sea. Today a busy commercial and industrial centre, with a shipyard and brewery, its origins are ancient and its historical and cultural associations many.

Egeskov Castle

It has been an episcopal residence since 1020 and St Knud's Cathedral, built in the mid 13th century, is a magnificent Gothic building with many interesting details, including a superb carved altarpiece with 300 figures by the Odense master Claus Berg. Knud (Canute) the Holy, of tide-commanding fame, was killed here and is buried in the fine crypt which also houses other royal tombs. Also of note is St Hans Church, begun in the 13th century.

Most famous of Odense's progeny was Hans Christian Andersen (1805–75), son of a shoemaker. His fairy tales enchanted the world and have been translated into over 100 languages. The house traditionally believed to be his birthplace has been restored and turned into a fascinating memorial, illustrating his life through letters, manuscripts, documents, pictures and other memorabilia. It includes the trunk of this lonely but much-travelled man, and the rope which he always carried with him as a means of escape in case of fire. Despite his nervousness and hypochondria, he undertook many hazardous journeys and met a galaxy of literary and aristocratic people as evidenced by his diaries and correspondence, among which are letters from Charles Dickens. Andersen fluctuated between delight and despair, yet he saw wonder in the workaday world and made others see it too. The humble house in which he lived until the age of 14 when he left for Copenhagen is also a museum. He loved children, but never married, though he had a deep love and friendship for Jenny Lind, the 'Swedish nightingale'. The Hans Christian Andersen Festival (mid July to mid August) is a delightful re-enactment of his fairy tales by the children of Odense.

Could he return, Andersen would recognize many of the buildings in Odense today. They include beautiful half-timbered houses, well represented in the museum of Møntrestraede, a collection of several 16th- and 17th-century buildings which illustrate the life of those times, including the history of the guild system. In the south part of town, Funen Village is a major open-air museum of old houses showing the peasant culture of the 18th and 19th centuries. Other museums of note are the Fyns Stifts Museum (archaeological finds from the Iron Age and an art collection focusing on Funen artists), the Kulturhistorisk Museum (relics from medieval times), the DSB Railway Museum (historic rolling stock and model railway), and the Falck Museum (fire and rescue vehicles). The 19th-century Town Hall is a striking building with a modern

Hans Christian Andersen's birthplace, Odense   *In Odense*

wing containing works of art. Odense's cultural life features its own symphony orchestra and an excellent theatre. There is a Tivoli pleasure garden.

Several interesting places in the surroundings include the childhood home of the composer Carl Nielsen at **Nr. Lyndelse** (16km/10mi S). The **Ladby** Viking Ship (16km/10mi E) is a remarkable find, set in a field near a half-timbered farm overlooking the fjord. Its ancient timbers sunk into the earth, the ship was the final resting place of a chieftain from about 850. The grave had been plundered, but the anchor and chain are there, and you can see the bones of animals which accompanied the chieftain on his last journey. This site could be combined with a visit to the church of **Rynkeby** whose 400-year-old frescoes show angels playing 32 different instruments from those times. *Esbjerg 137km/85mi.*

Rudkøbing   O8
(pop. 4800) This is the main town on the long island of Langeland, linked by causeway and bridge to Tåsinge and Funen. There are many charming old houses and the Langeland Museum contains collections from prehistory as well as depicting urban and peasant life in the 18th and 19th centuries. **Tranekaer** (12km/7mi NE) is a lakeside manor house, rebuilt many times, in a lovely park open to visitors. From Rudkøbing there are ferry services to the island of Strynø and to Marstal on Aerø; and from Bagenkop in south Langeland to Kiel, Germany. *Esbjerg 195km/121mi.*

Svendborg   N8
(pop. 25,000) This is an excellent spring-

board from which to tour the lovely south Funen countryside (especially by bicycle) and island-studded Svendborgsund, often alive with pleasure boats. Today a commercial and industrial town, it is also very picturesque with its older districts of half-timbered warehouses, cobbled streets and pretty cottages. The town also has a Regional Museum and Romanesque St Nikolaj Church. To the south, Svendborg is linked by bridge to the wooded island of Tåsinge. Here is the pretty little town of **Troense** whose Maritime Museum is housed in a late 18th-century school and has a splendid collection of model ships. In the nearby Baroque Valdemar Castle is a Naval Museum. The church of **Bregninge** on the main road to Langeland harbours a fine head of Christ from about 1200 and there are lovely views from Kirkebakken (Church Hill) over the islands. *Esbjerg 178km/110mi.*

SEALAND
MØN, FALSTER, LOLLAND

Sealand's most distinctive attributes are Copenhagen, Roskilde, the concentration (especially in north Sealand) of imposing palaces and castles, and the all-important Sound, the control of which has been such a dominant factor in Danish history. This is the most industrial part of Denmark, but there is still a lot of typical Danish countryside and coastline, with some of the most dramatic on the island of Møn.

Copenhagen see København

Frederikssund C7

(pop. 15,000) This modern industrial town at the narrowest point of Roskilde fjord developed from a fishing port whose ancient cottages can still be seen in the delightful Skyllebakke area near the harbour and shipyard. The J.F. Willumsen Museum is dedicated to the works of this great expressionist painter and sculptor. A major event is the Viking Festival (end June to early July), when local people re-create Viking life through plays based on Danish legends. The bridge across the fjord leads to the Hornsherred peninsula dotted with castles and churches, including **Jaegerspris**, a mansion mainly from the 16th–17th centuries, with royal memorabilia. *Copenhagen 40km/25mi.*

Helsingør/Elsinore B8

(pop. 55,000) This major seafaring and trading centre, with many ferry links to Helsingborg in Sweden across the narrow sound of Øresund, began its major development in the 15th century and much survives from its early days. The town centre is full of beautiful houses from the 16th–18th centuries, notably in Strandgade and Stengade streets. Famous Kronborg Castle, immortalized by Shakespeare in *Hamlet*, dominates the coast. It was built in the 16th century and rebuilt in its present Renaissance style after a fire in 1631. The interiors are splendid and include the uniquely preserved Chapel and huge Riddersalen (Knights' Hall). The Danish Maritime Museum is also housed here. Among other major sights are the Cathedral of St Olai (built 1480–1559), beautifully preserved Gothic St Maria Church and Monastery (wonderful cloisters; Baroque organ still in use), the Town Museum and Carmelite Monastery, Marienlyst Slot (historical museum in former summer palace). Two very fine collections are those of the Technical Museum of Denmark (science and transport) and the Øresund Aquarium.

In summer, a veteran railway links Helsingør with **Gilleleje** (24km/15mi) on Sealand's north coast, passing through the major seaside resort and sailing centre of **Hornbaek** (12km/7mi; superb beaches,

Kronborg Castle, Elsinore

innumerable summer cottages). At **Humlebaek** (10km/6mi S) is the notable Louisiana centre of art and culture dedicated to modern Danish and foreign art and set in a lovely park overlooking the Sound. Nearby is a museum to the composer Niels W. Gade. *Copenhagen 47km/29mi.*

Hillerød C8

(pop. 32,000) The town developed round Frederiksborg Castle, built in elaborate Dutch Renaissance style by Christian IV in 1600–20. After a fire in 1859, the castle was reconstructed according to the original plans, and has housed the National Historical Museum since 1878. The chapel, however, survived the fire; it is richly decorated with its altar and pulpit of ebony and silver, and a Compenius organ from 1610. This and the beautiful Knights' Hall head the list of Frederiksborg's considerable attractions, together with the magnificent Baroque gardens of the Castle Park. Other points of interest in Hillerød include the North Sealand Folk Museum in a charming 200-year-old thatched farm. At **Fredensborg** (9km/5mi NE) there is another castle. A gracious and more intimate building, used as the spring and autumn royal residence, Fredensborg Palace (Castle of Peace) was built in Italian style in 1722, following the Great Nordic War. The Park was created later in the 18th century on the lines of Versailles; one of its unusual features is Nordmandsdal, with 69 sandstone figures of Norwegian and Faroese fishermen in costume. From here it is only 15km/9mi NE to the most famous castle of all at Helsingør (above).

North west of Hillerød there are magnificent beaches by the pretty fishing hamlet of **Tisvildeleje** on Sealand's north coast. It is a distinctive landscape with attractive walks in Tisvilde Hegn, an area of shifting sands planted with woodland 200 years ago to halt erosion. The column of the Sand Drift Monument was erected at that time. A little inland is the 15th-century church of **Tibirke**, all that remains of a village engulfed by sand in the 18th century. *Copenhagen 36km/22mi.*

Kalundborg D5

(pop. 12,250) This industrial town on the west coast of Sealand has an important ferry harbour with services to Juelsminde and Århus in Jutland and to the island of Samsø. Its principal landmark is the massive 12th-century church with five towers. The town centre has a number of protected old buildings, one of which houses the museum. **Lerchenborg Castle** (5km/3mi S) is a Baroque manor

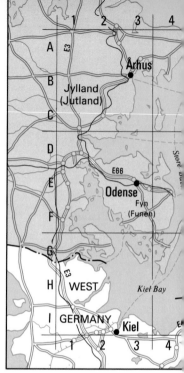

house set in a fine park. Concerts and other events take place in its Rococo Knights' Hall. *Copenhagen 100km/62mi.*

København/Copenhagen D8

(pop. 1,400,000) Regular car ferries link the Danish capital with Malmö in Sweden (also hydrofoils), Slite on Gotland, Oslo and Helsinki. As well as being a great industrial and seafaring port, Copenhagen is one of Europe's most graceful cities with its myriad copper spires and domes punctuating the skyline above the narrow streets and canals of the old town or poking up out of the greenery of its many parks. Of the first castle, built by Bishop Absalon in 1167, only the foundations remain in the cellars of Christiansborg Palace, seat of the Folketinget (Parliament), rebuilt for the third time on the same site in 1907–28. Copenhagen became the capital in 1415, but much of its expansion and several of its finest buildings date from the reign (1588–1648) of the energetic Christian IV. It has had its share of sieges and fires, and the majority of the oldest surviving buildings are from after the last great fire of 1795. Bombard-

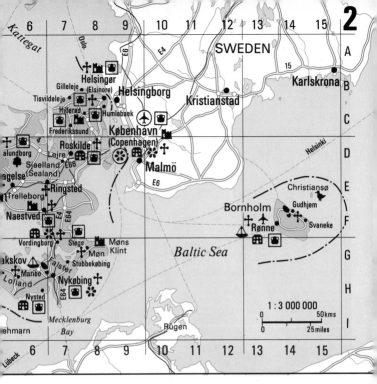

ment by the English in 1807, during Denmark's alliance with Napoleon, also caused much destruction. But there is still a great deal to see.

An efficient network of buses and electric trains serve the centre and suburbs. A joint zone fare system applies and you can interchange between bus and train routes using either a basic ticket (unlimited transfers within one zone and within one hour) or a tourist ticket valid for one day. There are also many daily sightseeing tours (various itineraries) round the city and into the surroundings by bus, and also canal and harbour trips.

Your best first port of call is the Tourist Information office at 2 Banegårdspladsen, by the Central Railway Station and Air Terminal; here you can get a wealth of free literature, maps and a copy of *Copenhagen This Week* telling you what's on, where and when. If you turn left into Vesterbrogade from here, you see Den Permanente (modern Danish arts and crafts) across the road and soon come to Vesterbrostorv and the Copenhagen City Museum (history, development and open-air model). If you turn right into

Vesterbrogade from the railway station you are within walking distance of a score of the city's main sights, the first of which is immediately on your right: far-famed Tivoli with its family entertainment from funfair thrills to sophisticated spectaculars and glorious gardens. Its ceremonial opening on 1 May marks the official beginning of summer.

To the left up Axeltorv is another famous Copenhagen fun spot, Benneweis Circus which opens about 1 April. Just beyond Tivoli is Tussaud's Wax Museum on the corner of Rådhus Pladsen (Town Hall Square), one of the principal hubs of the city from which many sightseeing tours begin, dominated by the turn-of-the-century Town Hall (famous Jens Olsen's World Clock) and the Lure Player Monument said to play every time a virgin passes! From here begins Strøget, Copenhagen's pedestrian-only shopping street, really a series of streets. It ends at Kongens Nytorv where you will find the Royal Theatre and Nyhavn, starting point for canal and harbour tours. About halfway along Strøget is the Church of the Holy Ghost (1730) bordering Gråbrodre-

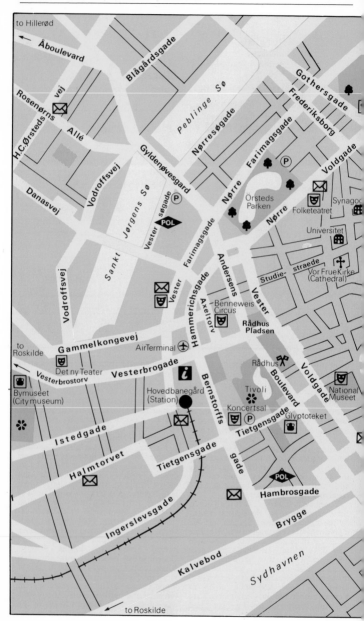

Kunst Museet

Botanisk Have

Sølv- voldgade

Mineralog. Museum

Øster-

Rosenborg Slot (Castle)

Rosenborg Have (Kongens Have)

Kronprinsessegade

Gothersgade

form urch

RundeTårn (Round Tower) Astronomical Collection

POL

trøget

Øster- gade

mmel Strand

Bremmerholm

Holmenskanal

horvaldsen Museum

Christiansborg

Teater Museet

(Royal Court Theatre)

Børsen

Royal Library

Christians Brygge

to E4 Helsingør

Fredericia- gade

POL

Frederiks Kirke (Marble Ch.)

Storekongens gade

Bredgade

Kongens Nytorv

Royal Theatre

Nyhavn

Holmenskirke

København (Copenhagen)

Churchill– parken

WorldWar II Museum

Kunstindustrimuseet (Museum of Decorative Art)

Amalienborg Slot (Palace)

N

Inderhavn

Strandgade

Torvegade

Amager Boulevard

Vermlandsgade

to Tarnby and airport

½ km

¼ mile

0
0

torv, a lively meeting place for the young, though the whole of Strøget presents an animated scene in summer, often with street musicians, theatres, protests, *etc*, in progress.

Many major sights can be reached by the narrow streets leading off Strøget. To the south you soon come to the attractive canal area of Gammel Strand. Across the canal is the Thorvaldsen Museum (dedicated to that great sculptor) and the massive complex of Christiansborg Palace, mentioned above, with adjacent Theatre History Museum in the Royal Court Theatre (1766) and Royal Stables (royal vehicles since 1778). Across the canal to the west is the 18th-century Prince's Palace housing the National Museum (fascinating collections ranging from prehistory to ethnography). East of Christiansborg, the Renaissance building on Christiansborg Castle Square with the distinctive dragons' tails spire is the Børsen (Stock Exchange), and across the canal the Renaissance Holmen's Church.

North of Strøget lie the neo-classical cathedral (1829), the main building of the university, the synagogue (consecrated 1833) and the Round Tower built in 1642 by Christian IV, its wide spiral' ramp leading up to the Observatory and Astronomical Collection. Continue north and you soon pass the Baroque Reform Church and come to Rosenborg Castle, another creation of Christian IV and once the royal country residence; today it houses rich treasures including the crown jewels.

To the west are the fine Botanical Gardens, a few blocks to the east the Marble Church (completed 1894 with imposing exterior statues) and the royal residence of Amalienborg Palace (1749–60) with daily Changing of the Guard at 1200. It is only a few minutes walk north from here to Langelinie and the famous bronze statué (1913) of the Little Mermaid, pensively observing the ships that come and go. On the way you can pass the Medical History Museum, Museum of Decorative Art and the World War II Resistance Museum in Churchill Park.

For Copenhagen's other great focus of family fun, you take the suburban train north to **Klampenborg** where Durehavsbakken (popularly known as 'Bakken'), Denmark's oldest amusement park, swings into action among the ancient oak trees in mid April. Adjoining it is the lovely Deer Park. To the west at nearby **Lyngby** is the excellent Open-Air Museum of Sorgenfri (old farms and houses, folk shows).

The city's night life is the liveliest and

(Background) Little Mermaid, Copenhagen

Royal Guard

Møns Klint

most varied in Scandinavia and its winter programmes range from music hall shows to the famous Royal Ballet. The big antique and art auctions are also fascinating. For sights near Copenhagen, see **Helsingør**, **Hillerød**, **Frederikssund** and **Roskilde**. *Copenhagen–Esbjerg 278km/172mi.*

Maribo   H5
(pop. 5300) Attractively placed by the Maribo lakes in the heart of the island of Lolland, this little town grew up round the abbey of which the 15th-century cathedral is part. The lakes offer a pleasant recreational area for walking and boating. A short distance north and accessible by veteran railway from Maribo is Scandinavia's largest manor house park of **Knuthenborg** with a famous safari park crossed by 16km/10mi of road. **Nysted** (pop. 1500; 24km/15mi SE) developed round Ålholm Castle, one of Europe's oldest inhabited castles (originally 12th century); nearby is northern Europe's biggest Veteran and Vintage Car Museum. **Nakskov** (pop. 17,500; 27km/15mi W) is beautifully placed on its fjord and has some well-preserved houses and warehouses. St Nikolaj church is late Gothic. From **Tårs**, a little to the north west, there is a regular ferry service to Langeland. *Copenhagen 136km/88mi.*

Møns Klint   G8
The beech-clad chalk cliffs on the east coast of the island of Møn offer one of the most startling landscapes in Denmark. They were formed 4000–5000 years ago, but the high hill complex of Høje Møn, of which they are part, was created about 20,000 years ago. It is composed of layers of Cretaceous chalk moulded out of the primeval ooze 75 million years back and studded with marine fossils, and glacial deposits from the actions of the last Ice Age. A footpath at the edge of the forest leads to many exotic formations. To the north is the charming Empire-style chateau of Liselund in a splendid English garden. **Stege** (20km/12mi W) is the main community on Møn and has a medieval town gate (Mølleporten), Møn Museum and St Hans Church with distinctive late 15th-century frescoes. *Copenhagen 123km/76mi.*

Naestved   F6
(pop. 46,000) This town in south Sealand developed round religious foundations and later became a major port for the booming Hanseatic trade. It is linked by canal to the sea. Today an industrial and garrison town, it still retains many fine old buildings, including Denmark's largest Gothic church, St Peter's, from the 13th–14th centuries. Naestved Museum

Roskilde Cathedral

in Helligåndshuset (1420) has a special section on leprosy. The important **Holmegård Glassworks** (8km/5mi NE), founded in 1825, can be visited. At **Sparresholm** (14km/8mi E), the stables of a 17th-century manor contain an interesting Carriage Museum. **Gavnø Castle** (7km/4mi SW) is a delightful Rococo creation with Denmark's largest privately owned art gallery and beautiful bulb gardens. *Copenhagen 82km/51mi.*

Nykøbing H7

(pop. 26,000) Principal town of Falster island, it is connected by bridge to the island of Lolland. The Gothic church is richly decorated and adjoins beautiful cloisters and monastery gardens with medicinal herbs. The District Museum is in a half-timbered house in which Peter the Great stayed in 1716. *Copenhagen 121km/75mi.*

Ringsted E7

(pop. 14,100) Situated in the centre of Sealand, this was an important town in medieval times. The brick Romanesque church of St Bendt was founded in the 12th century and contains the tomb of twelve medieval Danish kings. *Copenhagen 60km/37mi.*

Roskilde D7

(pop. 50,000) This has been a royal and episcopal residence since the 10th century. The cathedral, in Romanesque and Gothic styles, dates from the 1170s with later additions and houses dozens of Danish royal tombs, many of them magnificent works in marble and alabaster. Note that one of the figures at the foot of the sarcophagus of Christian IX in the chapel dedicated to him is of the same model as Copenhagen's Little Mermaid. There are also many memorial tablets, including beautiful examples of stonecutting from the Roskilde workshops from medieval times on. Connected to the cathedral by the 13th-century Absalon Arch is the Royal Mansion (1733). Roskilde's other great sights are to be found by the harbour in the Viking Ships Museum. Here you can see five remarkable vessels (dredged out of the fjord mud in 1962) which were deliberately sunk in the early 11th century to block enemy fleets approaching Roskilde, then an important trading town. Some of the vessels are still being painstakingly pieced together from the many thousands of pieces excavated from the sea.

Roskilde is a major centre for research and education and near **Lejre** (15km/9mi

Viking settlement, Trelleborg

SW) a most unusual piece of private research is in progress. Here at the Historical Archaeological Research Centre a scientific attempt to re-create conditions from the Iron Age is being carried out down to the last detail. This experiment in prehistoric living can be visited. In the same area the Baroque gardens of Ledreborg manor house (1744) are open to the public. Lejre village itself is an exquisite collection of half-timbered cottages. *Copenhagen 32km/19mi.*

Slagelse   E5
(pop. 33,000) This is a pleasant, busy commercial centre in the fertile region of west Sealand. Points of interest include St Mikkel Church in Gothic style and the ruins of Antvorskov monastery from the 12th century. An old church barn from the 16th century was at one time a grammar school, numbering Hans Christian Andersen among its pupils. **Trelleborg** (6km/4mi W) is one of the best-preserved Viking fortified circular encampments from the 11th century. The ground plan of the boat-shaped houses can be clearly seen and a full-size replica of one of them may be visited. *Copenhagen 89km/55mi.*

Vordingborg   G7
(pop. 11,600) This manufacturing and garrison town in southernmost Sealand

originally developed round the 12th-century castle of Valdemar the Great. The impressive castle ruins accommodate a Historical-Botanical garden (medicinal, spice and ornamental plants) and include a 700m/2300ft ring wall as well as the Goose Tower, Denmark's best-preserved medieval fortress tower. The church has a fine three-aisled interior with frescoes. The bridge linking Sealand with Falster is over 3km/2mi. *Copenhagen 92km/57mi.*

Bornholm   F14
(pop. 47,000) This Danish island in mid-Baltic roughly halfway between south Sweden and Poland has its own special and varied character. You can reach it by air or by sea, with regular ferries from Copenhagen, Travemünde (North Germany) and Ystad and Simrishamn (Sweden). Its 567sq km/220sq mi offer something of everything: great beaches of fine sand in the south, high cliffs in the north, a verdant hinterland of farmland, forests and heathery hills, unspoilt little townships with crooked streets and half-timbered cottages, ruined castles, runic stones and fortified round churches. Smoked herring is the island's chief delicacy.

The main town is **Rønne** (pop. 15,000) on the west coast, partly rebuilt after Russian bombing in 1945. The old district

Christiansø

round the church, opposite the yachting harbour, is charming. Note the Bornholm Museum, the Citadel on the town's southern outskirts and, 7km/4mi NE, the round church of **Nyker** with 14th-century frescoes. **Gudhjem** on the east coast is particularly pretty, its fig and mulberry trees and vines more reminiscent of the Mediterranean than the Baltic. From here a ferry serves the islet of **Christiansø** (50 mins), once a bastion of defence, now a magnet for seekers of peace, rare flora and varied bird life; other ferry services are from Sandvig/Allinge and Svaneke. The coast to the north of Gudhjem has the fabulous rock formations of **Helligdoms-Klipperne** while inland the Rø Plantation offers lovely scenery. To the east of this, and a short distance south of Gudhjem, is **Østerlars** with Bornholm's

oldest and largest fortified round church (impressive 14th-century frescoes).

Svaneke, further south on the east coast, has won a European Council award for its beautifully preserved unity. In the southern hinterland **Åkirkeby**'s church is an impressive medieval building with twin saddle roof and fine 12th-century font. To the east is the wild rock and heather country of **Paradisbakkerne**. But some of the most dramatic sights of all lie on the coast north of Rønne: the soaring rock formations of **Jons Kapel**, for example, and the rugged and romantic ruins of medieval clifftop **Hammershus Castle** near Bornholm's northern tip.

The island has particular appeal for artists, walkers, cyclists and bird-watchers for whom there are good facilities and special packages.

Faroe Islands

Faroe Islands   B2

(The Faroes appear on Map 1, p. 33.)
The 18 islands of the Faroes make up a
self-governing region under the Danish
kingdom. They cover an area of 1399sq
km/540sq mi, have a population of 42,000
and lie roughly halfway between the Shet-
lands and Iceland. Originally discovered
by Irish monks in the 8th century, they
were colonized by Norsemen about 800
and adopted Christianity in 1000. In 1035
they were attached to Norway and, with
the latter, became united in due course
with Denmark. When this union ended in
1814, the islands remained Danish; the
present state of autonomy dates from
1948.

The Faroes' isolated position, buffeted
often by the inclement moods of the North
Atlantic, has contributed to the survival,
unadulterated, of much of the islanders'
cultural heritage. The Faroese language,
for example, derives from ancient Norse
and is most closely related to Icelandic.
You can get there quite easily by air or by
sea, but it presupposes a certain singleness
of purpose for the islands are not readily
combined with anywhere else, other than
Iceland, although they do feature on a few
cruise itineraries. Their great claims for
attention are their spectacular coastal
scenery, their remarkable bird life, some
good angling and an unspoilt and un-
complicated way of life.

Only 6 per cent of the land is cultivated,
the rest providing rough grazing for the
sheep which outnumber the population
by nearly two to one in winter and form an
important part of the islanders' economy,
clothing (woven or beautifully hand-
knitted woollen goods) and diet. Much
more significant, however, are the fisheries and the fish-processing industries
which provide the overwhelming propor-

tion of the Faroes' income. Mutton and
fish, both air-dried and often eaten with
unleavened bread, form a big part of the
national diet. Guillemot and puffin meat
are among local delicacies. There is no
alchohol for sale on the islands.

The largest and most central island is
Streymoy and on it is the capital **Tórshavn** (pop. 11,600). Here met the ancient Parliament on the hill of Tinganes
from about 900; today it is housed in
attractive well-preserved timber buildings. Sights include Skansin fortress (the
present one dates from the 1780s), the
grass-roofed houses of the older districts,
and several museums devoted to Faroese
archaeology, ethnography, natural history
and seafaring traditions.

Transport round the islands is a combination of scheduled minibuses, taxis and
ferries. The cliff scenery, in many places
rearing to 300–600m/1000–2000ft out of
the sea, with marine stacks and caves, is
enormously dramatic and some stretches
carry tumultuous populations of puffins,
kittiwakes, guillemots, fulmars, gulls and
shearwaters. Many species of duck and
wader are to be found, too, among them
the oystercatcher which is the Faroes'
protected national bird. Local advice
should be sought on the best areas and
means of getting to them.

As in Iceland, the landscapes of the
Faroes have strong associations with early
sagas and their heroes, which give an
added dimension to the wild beauty. In a
number of places, old farms have been
excavated and, in some cases (*eg* at Saksun
on Streymoy) restored and equipped in
every detail to illustrate conditions from
medieval times onwards. The Faroes'
second largest community is **Klaksvík**
(pop. 4600) on Bordoy, a lively centre for
the activities of the Faroese fishing fleets.

FINLAND

Of Finland's total land frontiers of 2547km/1583mi, 538/335 are shared with Sweden, 733/456 with Norway and 1276/793 with the USSR. Her 1107km/688mi of coastline ranges from the Gulf of Bothnia in the west, the Baltic in the south west and Gulf of Finland in the south. The sea is broken up by tens of thousands of islands and skerries; the land is fragmented by tens of thousands of lakes, and, in some regions, divided by long parallel lines of low ridges left by the retreat of the last Ice Age. Indeed, 9 per cent of the land is covered by inland waters, and this rises to 50 per cent in the great lake districts of the south east; over 70 per cent is forest, the main agricultural areas being concentrated in the flat plains of the west. Dotted about these lake-and-forestscapes are the communities that have grown into townships, mostly originating as small industrial centres drawing their raw materials from the 'green gold' of the surrounding forests. The further north you travel the more sparsely scattered are the communities; but they are never lacking in modern buildings or the latest amenities, and some of the best examples of new architecture are to be found in the remotest places.

Ethnically, the Finns are the odd ones out in the Nordic countries. Except for the 6 per cent who speak Swedish as their mother tongue, they belong to a different linguistic group (p. 30) and, acting as a buffer state between alien cultures over the centuries, they acquired influences from two directions. From Russia and the east came the Orthodox faith which still has a substantial minority following, and such culinary items as *bortsch* (beetroot soup with sour cream), *blini* (pancake with smetana sour cream) and vodka (the Finns consider they produce the best). But by far the greatest influence came via the south west from Sweden, part of which Finland formed for about 600 years. This was the route taken by the dominant western church which resulted in the many medieval stone churches still to be seen in the south west today; and this was the route of the arts and manners of Europe, as well as a rather peaceful Reformation and, in due course, democracy.

Finland's huge and beautiful outdoors makes it a natural setting for open-air activities of all kinds. The Finns love to escape from their well-run cities at every opportunity and nearly all own or rent a summer cottage which can range from a simple hut to a minor mansion. Set in the heart of forests on river, lake or seashore, it is an idyllic retreat from which to go boating, fishing, swimming, walking, picking berries, or just to contemplate from a granite boulder under a huge sky. You can do the same. This taste for simplicity is often combined with a profound interest in the literature, music and art of the world, which accounts for art centres in the heart of the countryside and a series of excellent cultural festivals punctuating the summer calendar (see gazetteer).

Probably the most famous Finnish speciality is the sauna (see also p. 23) which you will find in almost every hotel, hostel, campsite, holiday village and most private homes. The basic principle is one of dry heat which is why the body can withstand temperatures of 100°C/212°F and more. The heat comes from a stove in a corner of the sauna, nowadays usually heated electrically, but ideally by wood; this is topped by a pile of baking hot stones on which a small amount of water is thrown from time to time, adding moisture to the air and giving the illusion of a sharp rise in temperature. The best sauna is usually a small pine log cabin on a lake or seashore. The usual practice in a private sauna after sweating it out, is to wash and shower or plunge into sea or lake, then repeat the process as often as desired, usually rounding off with quiet relaxation and a cold drink on the balcony overlooking the water (in winter a hardy few roll in the snow or dip into a hole in the ice). Hotel or public saunas often impose a time limit, though there is sometimes a place to relax and take refreshment afterwards, an essential part of the process which is social as well as cleansing. In the old days, the sauna was usually built before the living quarters of a house, and it was considered a cure for almost all imaginable ills.

For communities with a substantial Swedish-speaking minority, the Swedish

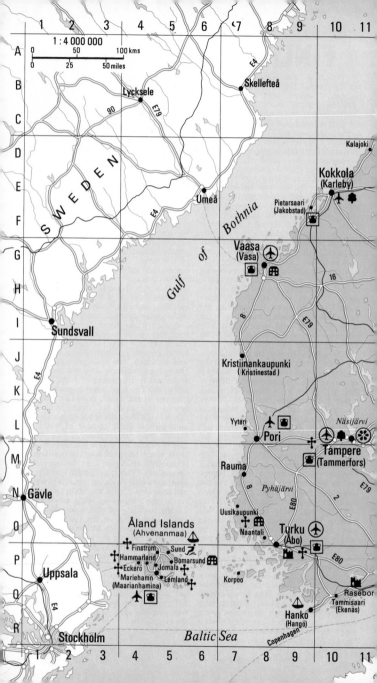

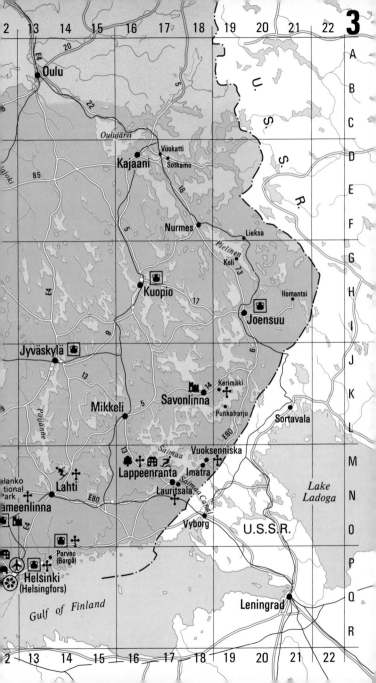

name is given after the Finnish in the following gazetteer. The exception is Åland, where the population is almost entirely Swedish-speaking and therefore the Finnish name is given after the Swedish.

SOUTH FINLAND

Åland Islands/ Ahvenanmaa   P5

(pop. 22,000) This scattering of over 6500 islands and skerries dotted about 10,000sq km/3860sq mi of sea makes up the autonomous province of Åland. 'Stepping stones' between Sweden and Finland, they were for a time a bone of contention between the two countries, but Finland's sovereignty was recognized by the League of Nations in 1921. The population, however, is almost entirely Swedish-speaking; they have their own flag, their own laws, and an ancient seafaring tradition which included some of the most famous sailing ships to travel the seven seas. Here are traces of countless prehistoric settlements, Viking graves and the remains of the oldest churches in Finland. Here, too, is an idyllic summer playground particularly well geared for sailing, other water sports and cycling and there is a wonderful rural calm to be enjoyed from a well-organized network of hotels, guest houses and self-catering cottages. Fishing and especially farming are main occupations, but Åland still has a merchant fleet out of all proportion to its size.

Mariehamn/Maarianhamina (pop. 9500) is the capital and the only town, a miniature garden city in summer with a profusion of flowers and leafy linden trees. It straddles a narrow peninsula, its main thoroughfares, Norra Esplanadgatan and Storagatan, linking the east and west harbours, about 2km/1mi apart. You can learn much about the archipelago – still growing at the rate of about ½m/2ft a century out of the sea – at the Ålands Museum. The Maritime Museum, West Harbour, has splendid displays of relics from famous windjammers; alongside is the museum ship, the four-masted barque *Pommern*.

Though the outer islands are rocky and rugged, the main island is extremely pretty, crisscrossed by narrow but well-surfaced lanes. The interesting restored castle of **Kastelholm** (25km/15mi NE of Mariehamn) was built by the Swedes in the 14th century, while the adjoining farm museum of Jan Karlsgården re-creates the islands' peasant culture. At **Bomarsund** (35km/21mi NE) are the ruins of a vast

naval fortress begun by the Russians and destroyed by Anglo-French forces in the Crimean War. Two of the finest medieval stone churches with wall paintings are at **Jomala** (7km/4mi N) and **Finström** (25km/15mi N). Other churches include **Hammarland** (21km/13mi NW), **Eckerö** (37km/23mi NW), **Sund** (25km/15mi NE) and **Lemland** (13km/8mi SE). The ruins of 13th-century **Lemböte Chapel** enjoy a fine setting near one of the largest Viking cemeteries in the archipelago. Numerous sea and air services link Åland with Sweden and mainland Finland.

Hämeenlinna   N12

(pop. 42,000) This small country town was the birthplace of Jean Sibelius whose childhood home is now one of several museums. Modern buildings have replaced most of the wooden houses of the past, but the local castle (restored) is a worthy medieval pile and can be visited. The most famous of several medieval greystone churches in the area is that of **Hattula** (7km/4mi N), its interior entirely covered with early 16th-century frescoes in excellent condition. **Aulanko National Park** (3km/2mi N) is a fine civilized wilderness of artificial lakes and imported trees with a top-class hotel offering sports facilities. Hämeenlinna is the southern terminal of the popular Silver Line lake route (several hours) from Tampere (p. 61). *Helsinki 104km/64mi.*

Hanko/Hangö   Q9

(pop. 12,000) At the tip of a long peninsula on the Gulf of Finland, this is the best-known south-coast summer resort for bathing and especially sailing. **Tammisaari/Ekenäs** (36km/22mi NE) is a charming little seaside town with the ruined medieval castle of Raseborg in the vicinity. *Helsinki 126km/78mi.*

Helsinki/Helsingfors   P12

(pop. 500,000) Until 1812, Helsinki was an unimportant little market town near the mouth of the River Vantaa. Czar Alexander I made it the new capital (see also Turku) and the present elegant district round the cathedral and South Harbour, created by J.A. Ehrenström and Carl Ludvig Engel, dates largely from the 1830s. The main part of the city fills a peninsula which is linked by bridges, causeways and boat services to its widespread suburbs and satellite towns. But even in the centre, the glint of the sea is round almost every corner, and the natural rock and trees are part of the urban scene.

Helsinki Guide and other free publi-

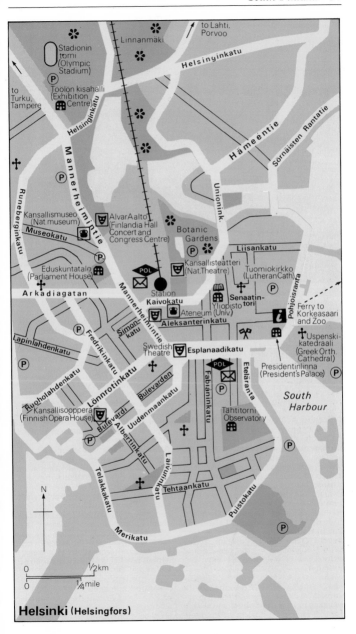

Helsinki (Helsingfors)

Sibelius monument

(Background) Helsinki

cations give the latest details of what's on, when and where. Public transport is by tramcar and bus; you can buy a Tourist Ticket giving unlimited travel on the central network for 24 hours. An excellent route for orientation is the 3T tram, which describes a rough figure-eight through the city, bringing you back to your starting point. The new underground train system, probing deep into the city's granite foundations, is a technological marvel.

You can pick up the 3T by the South Harbour, which is high on the list of Helsinki's attractions, with its open-air morning market, all year and whatever the weather, selling fresh fish, flowers, fruit and vegetables as well as handicrafts and household goods. Regular and sightseeing boats set out from here to the islands, and several main shipping routes have their terminals here. Overlooking the harbour are the red-brick Uspenski Orthodox Cathedral, the President's Palace and Town Hall and nearby are the City Tourist Office and the elegant Senate Square dominated by the neo-classical architecture of the cathedral and other buildings.

The parklike boulevard, Esplanaadi-katu, running west from the South Harbour, is where you find the displays and shops of several fashion and design firms. It ends at the Swedish Theatre on

the main artery of Mannerheimintie. Parallel with Esplanaadikatu to the north is Aleksanterinkatu, linking the cathedral with the commercial hub of the city and, via side streets, with the main Railway Station and its square where you also find the National Theatre, the Ateneum Art Gallery, and the Central Post Office which stands on the corner of Mannerheimintie. From here you can see the handsome colonnaded red-granite Parliament building and, further north, the churchlike tower of the National Museum almost opposite the imposing modern Finlandia Hall (Concert and Congress Centre by Alvar Aalto). Further north still is the Olympic Stadium (fine view tower) and International Fair Centre (1975), a complex of exhibition halls and well-planned open spaces.

Several main Helsinki sights are on islands. There is Seurasaari with its open-air museum of buildings from all over the country, and summer theatre; Korkeasaari with its zoo; Suomenlinna, once called the 'Gibraltar of the North', with its 18th-century fortifications on a series of islands, now being turned into a centre for leisure and the arts.

A gem of modern architecture is Tempeliaukio Church, built out of the living rock in the Töölö district; but modern architecture is a feature in all of greater Helsinki, with Tapiola Garden City as the

Lake Saimaa

most famous example. Sightseeing tours of the city, the suburbs and out-of-town destinations begin from the bus station on Simonkatu. Recommended shorter trips are to **Ainola** (home of Sibelius) and **Hvitträsk** where the former home of three great architects is a charming lakeside museum and leisure centre, with nearby Stone Age rock paintings. See also **Hämeenlinna** and **Porvoo**.

There is plenty of fairly expensive night life, open-air theatres and concerts, and Linnanmäki pleasure gardens is a fun place for the family. The Helsinki Festival is a major arts event in late August and early September.

Joensuu   I20
(pop. 45,000) This pleasant provincial town is one of the terminals of the Saimaa lake fleet and mainly of interest as the gateway to the unspoilt lake-and-forest country of North Karelia. Karelia House includes an interesting museum of the region's culture. The **Koli Heights** (347m/1138ft) are the highest point (75km/46mi N) above Lake Pielinen, with astounding views over vast areas of waterlaced forests. There are good hotel and self-catering facilities, and amenities for outdoor activities down by the lake. Regular boat services on Pielinen link Joensuu, Lieksa, Koli and Nurmes in summer.

Nurmes, at the northern end of Pielinen (125km/77mi), is a very pretty small town with many wooden houses. East of Joensuu, **Ilomantsi** (73km/45mi) is in the heart of the unspoilt and predominantly Orthodox border country with the Soviet Union and here a strong folk tradition has survived. The Pradznik or Praasniekka Orthodox Festivals are very colourful events at several places in summer, especially at Ilomantsi in mid June. *Helsinki 469km/291mi.*

Jyväskylä   J14
(pop. 63,000) At the northern end of the Päijänne lake system in central Finland, Jyväskylä has a long tradition as an educational centre. Its university was designed by Alvar Aalto. The Alvar Aalto Museum and the Museum of Central Finland, with handicrafts and workers' cottages, are the most interesting collections. Just outside the town is the important sports complex centred on Laajavuori Hill. The forests to the north are dotted with many holiday villages offering hotels or self-catering facilities and various outdoor activities. The Jyväskylä Arts Festival is a major cultural event focusing on a different theme each year (end June to early July). Regular steamer and hydrofoil services link Jyväskylä and Lahti (below). *Helsinki 276km/171mi.*

Lahti

Kajaani D16
(pop. 34,000) The town's main attraction is as the doorway to the magnificently wild landscapes of Kainuu. It is built in the shelter of a now-ruined castle and was once Europe's greatest exporter of tar. It was while working here as a doctor that Elias Lönnrot collected the material that eventually became the Finnish national epic, *Kalevala* (p. 11). Eastwards lies a chain of lakes stretching to the Soviet border, with splendid facilities for outdoor activities, winter and summer, at **Sotkamo** (41km/25mi) and, near it, Vuokatti. *Helsinki 566km/351mi.*

Kuopio H16
(pop. 75,000) This is the northern terminal for Saimaa lake traffic. From the tower on Puijo Hill the views are superb. The town has winding old narrow streets and the collections in the Orthodox Church Museum are unique in western Europe. The Kuopio Dance and Music Festival is a lively event in June. *Helsinki 392km/243mi.*

Lahti N14
(pop. 100,000) This modern city is best known as a ski centre and was the scene of the World Ski Championships in 1978. It lies between the two ridges of Salpausselkä on Vesijärvi, the southern end of the Päijänne lake system which links Lahti by boat and hydrofoil services to Jyväskylä. The huge ski jump, modern architecture and sculptures are Lahti's main features, notably the Church of the Cross (Ristinkirkko) designed by Aalto in the town centre. In contrast, the old church and museum of **Hollola**

(16km/10mi NW) are also interesting. An international Organ Festival is held in August. *Helsinki 103km/63mi.*

Lappeenranta N17
(pop. 54,000) Lappeenranta is the southern terminal for Saimaa lake traffic and the northern terminal for summer cruises to Vyborg (Viipuri) and Leningrad in the Soviet Union (visas essential) via the **Saimaa Canal**, once an important commercial link with the Gulf of Finland. Since 1944 over half the canal has been in Soviet territory but, after long negotiations, it was restored and reopened in 1968. There are also short cruises on the Finnish section of the canal (without visa). The town is a popular lake resort as well as a timber centre, with good facilities for excursions and water sports. Substantial remains survive of the fort and old entrenchments from the days when it was alternately a Finnish and a Russian garrison town, and these now form part of a park with open-air summer theatre. Here, too, is the Orthodox Church (1785). The open-air market in the town centre is a lively spot. Two fine modern churches in the area are that of Taivaan Talo at **Lauritsala** (5km/3mi E) and the Church of Three Crosses by Alvar Aalto at **Vuoksenniska** near Imatra (37km/23mi NE). At **Imatra**, the rapids of Imatrankoski were once one of the great natural beauties of Finland. Their power has been harnessed, but is released in full splendour on certain Sundays in summer. *Helsinki 221km/137mi.*

Pietarsaari/Jakobstad F9
(pop. 20,500) This rather attractive small

Castle at Savonlinna

coastal town is an air and sea-traffic centre for connections across the northern Gulf of Bothnia to Sweden. Tobacco is the oldest of its several industries (there is a Tobacco Museum), but there are also strong cultural associations, notably with Finland's national poet, J.L. Runeberg, born here in 1804. His school and his father's cottage are both museums. A scenic road leads through the archipelago to **Kokkola/Karleby** (38km/23mi NE) a pleasant town of whitewashed houses. A curiosity is the English landing craft captured in the Crimean War, on display in English Park. **Kalajoki** (102km/63mi N) is a place for beach addicts: a superb stretch of rolling dunes, with varied accommodation and sports facilities. *Helsinki 500km/310mi.*

Pori   L8
(pop. 80,000) The sea has receded so that the major port of Pori at **Mäntyluoto** is now 20km/12mi NW from the centre of this modern industrial town. The Satakunta Museum is one of the largest regional museums in Finland. The annual International Jazz Festival takes place in July on an island in the river. Near the port one of the best beaches on the Baltic is **Yyteri**, now a tourist resort. Punctuating this stretch of coast are some of Finland's prettiest towns in which districts of old wooden houses bordering leafy narrow streets still survive. They include **Rauma** (50km/31mi S) and **Kristiinankaupunki/Kristinestad** (100km/62 mi N). *Helsinki 243km/150mi.*

Porvoo   P14
(pop. 20,000) The old part of the town is a picture-book place with brightly painted old wooden houses from the 16th–18th centuries. It is an important publishing centre and has attracted artists and writers for generations. The 15th-century cathedral has interesting frescoes, and a statue of Alexander I is a reminder that here he appointed Finland's first ever national legislative assembly in 1809. The home of J.L. Runeberg, Finland's national poet, is among several museums; another is the Art Museum devoted to 19th-century sculptor Ville Valgren and painter Albert Edelfelt. *Helsinki 50km/31mi.*

Savonlinna   K18
(pop. 28,300) Situated in the very heart of the Saimaa lake district, Savonlinna is a timber centre and a holiday resort with good facilities as well as being the hub of regular boat services in every direction. On summer mornings and evenings, the quayside is ever busy with the comings and goings of lake traffic which moors here overnight. Olavinlinna, built in 1475 to protect the shifting eastern frontier, is one of the best medieval castles in Scandinavia, and scene of an annual Opera Festival in July. The surrounding deeply forested countryside is beautiful, and the narrow ridge of **Punkaharju** (30km/18mi SE) is a famous beauty spot. **Kerimäki** (24km/15mi E) has Europe's largest wooden church (1847). *Helsinki 334km/207mi.*

Tampere/Tammerfors   L11
(pop. 170,000) Finland's second city has grown astride the rapids of Tammerkoski on an isthmus between the big lakes of

Näsijärvi and Pyhäjärvi. Although it has a concentration of industry, Tampere is also a city of the theatre and the arts and its situation makes it a holiday centre in its own right. A Scotsman, James Finlayson, built the first cotton mill here in 1820, and it remains Finland's leading textile centre. Today a line of factories borders the tamed rapids, but green spaces are just as much a feature of the city. The biggest park is Pyynikki and its lakeside open-air theatre has the world's first revolving auditorium. Just across the isthmus in the park of Särkänniemi is a Funfair and Recreation Centre dominated by Näsinneula Observation Tower (168m/550ft) which houses a planetarium, aquarium and children's zoo.

The city's excellent museums and art galleries include the Sara Hildén Art Museum (modern, highly imaginative), the Häme Museum (excellent regional collection), the Technical Museum (all types of vehicles over the centuries), a charming Doll and Costume Museum, and the Lenin Museum (it was here that Lenin and Stalin first met). The cathedral in National Romantic style (1902–7, Sonck) has some famous paintings, among them Hugo Simberg's macabre *Garden of Death*. In contrast, Kaleva Church (1966, Pietilä) is controversially modern, while the surrounding countryside has a number of well-preserved medieval stone churches, including that of **Messukylä** (5km/3mi SE). The city has many fine sculptures, notably by Wäinö Aaltonen (traditional) and Eila Hiltunen (modern). The annual Tampere Theatre Summer occurs in August. Tampere is the northern terminal for the Silver Line lake route from Hämeenlinna (p. 56), and southern terminal for the Poet's Way boat tour to Virrat (7½ hours). *Helsinki 176km/110mi.*

Turku/Åbo   O8
(pop. 165,000) This is Finland's most ancient city and was her capital until 1812 when Czar Alexander I considered it too far from St Petersburg for security and chose Helsinki instead. It is still a major administrative and educational centre, and is Finland's most important year-round ice-free port with many sea and air links to Sweden. There are two universities, one teaching in Finnish, one in Swedish; the former is a striking example of modern architecture. It is a restful city, with the River Aura winding through the centre fringed by little boats and bordered by parks whose trees frame the distinctive single tower of the cathedral. This is one of Turku's three most famous sights, originally completed at the end of the 13th century, but damaged, restored or ex-

tended over the centuries. Many notable historical figures are buried here. The two other major sights are the medieval but restored castle, close to the harbour, housing a fine Historical Museum; and the Luostarinmäki Handicraft Museum, a street of old houses that survived the great fire of 1827, now a charming open-air museum peopled in summer with craftsmen demonstrating their skills.

Many of the older districts of Turku have been rebuilt; some of the more striking modern buildings along the river include the City Theatre, the Wäinö Aaltonen Museum (partly devoted to Finland's most famous sculptor) and the Sibelius Museum. There is a lively morning market on the big square of Kauppatori, and a second-hand market in Aninkaistentori. Two notable modern churches are the Resurrection Chapel (1941, Bryggman) and Chapel of the Holy Cross (1967, Pitkänen). **Ruissalo**, 10km/6mi W of the city, is a lovely park with golf and other sports facilities.

Between Turku and the Åland islands (p. 56), thousands more islands and skerries rise out of the sea, some linked by a series of bridges, causeways and ferries, others by boat services, to the mainland, providing a wide variety of excursions. The road to **Korpoo**, necessitating several ferries, is one recommendation. Seven medieval churches in Turku's surrounding countryside offer the theme of another tour. The small towns of **Naantali** (16km/10mi NW) with its 15th-

Naantali bridge

century Convent Church and the presidential summer residence, and **Uusikaupunki** (78km/48mi NW) are especially picturesque. The annual Turku Music Festival takes place in August. *Helsinki 167km/104mi.*

Vaasa/Vasa   G8
(pop. 54,000) This is the main west-coast centre for sea and air connections across the Gulf of Bothnia to Sweden. It was the headquarters of the White Guards in the War of Independence against the Red Guards in 1918. After a devastating fire in

1852, the new town was moved closer to the receding sea; remains of old Vaasa (churches, castle, a museum) can be seen on the original site at Mustasaari. In the modern town, the Ostrobothnian Museum has good regional collections and the Brage Open-Air Museum at Hietalahti is a collection of old farm buildings. There are also delightful island trips by waterbus. *Helsinki 415km/257mi.*

NORTH FINLAND

This section deals mainly with the northernmost province of Lappi (Finnish Lapland) stretching from just south of the Arctic Circle almost to the Arctic Ocean, but it also includes the northern city of Oulu and the fell district of Rukatunturi, both of which lie outside the boundaries of Lappi.

Until World War II, much of it was a trackless wilderness, but war brought new roads, armies and eventually devastation. Much of the area was destroyed by retreating German armies in 1944. Since then sophisticated pockets of civilization have multiplied and roads have probed ever further into the forests and tundra. Yet, though the region is now easily accessible and offers every modern comfort, silent primeval landscapes wait unchanged just round the corner for those willing and equipped to enjoy them. Forests, swamps, swift streams and bareheaded fells are the chief characteristics of these landscapes, plus countless lakes some of which are immense. The trees become more and more stunted as latitude and altitude increase. Eventually conifers are left behind and then forests of dwarf birch finally give way to the miniscule vegetation of the tundra.

Economically, Lappi is a poor province. There is some light industry in the south, but the economy is mainly based on forestry and reindeer breeding. Most of the year, the reindeer roam free, but they are counted, marked or slaughtered once a year at colourful reindeer roundups, usually in late autumn and winter when zipping lassoes and pounding hooves conjure up a Wild West film in an Arctic setting. But you need to check 'when' and 'where' on the spot. Of Lappi's 200,000 inhabitants, only about 3500 are Lapps – or Same (pronounced Saa-me), as these proud people prefer to be called (see also pp. 91, 118). Few now wear the bright traditional costumes, except on special occasions such as church festivals; and only a very few families follow the reindeer herds on seasonal migration. Most have settled in small homesteads, many

have taken up a trade or profession, and the youngsters mostly indulge in the same tastes and pursuits as youngsters elsewhere. Note that the Same people of northern Finland include a small group with quite different cultural features. They are the Skolt Lapps who historically were influenced by the Russians and other peoples to the east; they follow the Orthodox faith and have their own traditions. Most live in the Ivalo area or in the remote settlement of Sevettijärvi in the north east.

Two main roads and a network of minor ones, most of them served by regular bus, send their threads across the Lappi map. Daily air services reach to Ivalo, nearly 300km/186mi north of the Arctic Circle. The best way to experience Lappi is to choose one or two centres and then walk – you will learn nothing from a few days speeding along its roads. But you should never venture far alone in the wilderness unless you are experienced, and always tell someone where you are going and when you expect to be back. In summer be prepared for large numbers of mosquitoes, though some years are worse than others.

Spring (late May–June), following the retreat of a long, tough winter, is an exhilarating time to visit Lappi; in autumn (from early September) the colours are so spectacular that the Finns have a special word for it: *ruskaa.* There is superb cross-country skiing in winter and early spring, the latter's lengthening days and clear air producing enviable suntans. The shifting coloured veils of the Northern Lights sweeping the sky in the darker months are quite unforgettable.

Enontekiö   F5

One of the most attractive of the Lappi church villages, Enontekiö (old name Hetta) is scattered along the northern

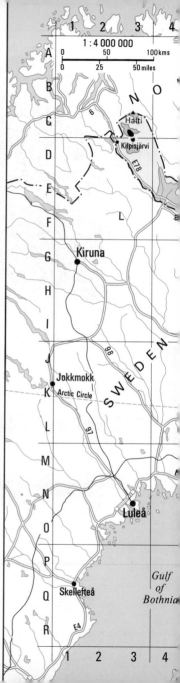

shore of narrow Ounasjärvi lake from whose southern shore rise the Ounasturi fells crossed by a marked hiking trail (p. 66). It lies 26km/16mi east of highway 21 and also has road links northwards with Norway. As the main village for an enormous area, its attractive modern church and other amenities serve scattered communities of the Same people. *Rovaniemi 315km/195mi.*

Inari   E9

This community on the south-west shore of huge Lake Inari is an important centre for the Same people from a wide area, and colourful weddings and sports events take place here, usually at Easter or Lady Day. There are also many winter reindeer roundups in the surrounding wilderness. In summer, excursions on the island-studded lake, fishing and hiking are the main attractions. There is an interesting Same Museum in the village from which a marked trail (15km/9mi return) leads to a remote 18th-century wooden church at Pielppäjärvi. Other marked hiking trails start from **Njurgalahti** (46km/28mi SW), a Same community in the Lemmenjoki river goldwashing area, and some guided trips are arranged. *Rovaniemi 335km/209mi.*

Lapp, Lake Inari

Ivalo   E10

On the banks of Ivalojoki river and astride highway 4, this large village is a main traffic and trading centre for northern Lappi, with Finland's northernmost airport. Its proximity to Inari and the extensive and wild **Saariselkä** fells are its main tourist attractions. The latter lie to the south of Ivalo and east of highway 4, and are serviced by a number of tourist centres accessible by road; there is a number of marked hiking trails. A minority Same group, the Skolt Lapps (p. 63), live in the Ivalo area. *Rovaniemi 295km/183mi.*

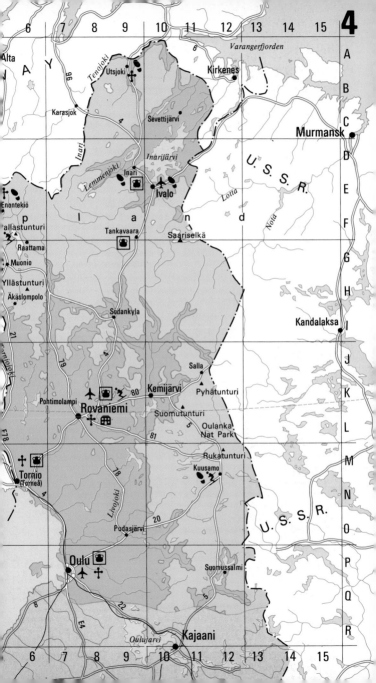

Kilpisjärvi D2

Near the tip of the north-western arm of Finland, Kilpisjärvi and its lake lie close to the border with Sweden and Norway. Indeed, the boundary stone where the three countries meet, to the north west, is a popular destination for walkers, 24km/15mi from the hotel. A marked trail leads to it via Malla Nature Reserve with its varied and protected flora (permit needed, available from the excursion centre or tourist hotel); or you can do most of the journey by boat across the lake. The village is dominated by Saana fell (1029m/3375ft) once considered holy by the Same people; the very easy climb is rewarded by superb views. Beyond it, the extensive roadless wilderness merges into Norway and includes Finland's highest fell, Halti (1328m/4356ft). *Rovaniemi 440km/273mi.*

Kuusamo M12

Kuusamo, on highway 5, is the nearest village to the splendid **Rukatunturi** fell district (25km/15mi N). Here you will find varied accommodation in a magnificently wild setting, and amenities for summer hiking and winter skiing. The popular marked trail known as the Bear Circuit (55km/34mi, but shorter variations possible) links Rukatunturi with Kiutaköngas to the north across the high forested hills of Oulanka National Park, ribbed by deep valleys and racing rivers. From Rukatunturi you can also shoot the rapids with an expert through a nearby canyon. *Helsinki 833km/517mi, Rovaniemi 195km/121mi.*

Oulu P7

(pop. 95,000) This lively northern city was one of the world's most important tar export harbours in the 19th century; today it concentrates on timber, paper and chemical products. Oulu grew round the Merikoski rapids whose waters feed the big power station designed by Alvar Aalto. The busy riverside Market Square is overlooked by the city's ultramodern theatre and a contrasting group of preserved ancient salt storehouses. Other points of interest include the cathedral (1845, Engel), the North Ostrobothnian Museum in Ainola Park and the open-air museum on Turkansaari, an island in the river (13km/8mi E). *Helsinki 617km/382mi.*

Pallastunturi F5

The tourist complex here takes its name from a group of 14 fells and lies 31km/19mi E of Muonio on highway 79. It is magnificent fell-walking (and skiing) country with a marked hiking trail from the hotel over the Pallastunturi and Ounastunturi fells to Enontekiö (64km/40mi N; p. 63). In some of the small communities of the area, such as **Raattama** and **Ylikyrö**, very old wooden houses survived war destruction because of their remoteness, but are now accessible by a minor road which provides an attractive alternative route to Enontekiö. *Rovaniemi 260km/161mi.*

Rovaniemi L8

(pop. 30,000) Rovaniemi was almost totally destroyed by the retreating German army in 1944, and was rebuilt according to plans by Alvar Aalto. It stands at the junction of the Kemi and Ounas rivers, only a few miles south of the Arctic Circle. The modern architecture and amenities of this administrative capital of the province of Lappi come as a surprise to those expecting a backwoods town. It has excellent hotels, varied shops and is the gateway for air and road traffic throughout Lappi. Lappia House is the civic centre complex designed by Aalto, housing the theatre, concert hall, and the Lapland Provincial Museum. A little outside town are the Ethnographic and Forestry Museums at Pöykkölä. The modern parish church has a huge altar fresco *The Source of Life* (L. Segerstråle). Rising out of the town are the Ounasvaara hills which give their name to the annual international ski championships in March. **Pohtimolampi** Sports and Excursion Centre (28km/17mi NW) has the world's only reindeer driving school. *Helsinki 850km/528mi.*

Tankavaara F9

A short distance from highway 4 lies this unusual museum run by the association of gold prospectors in Finnish Lapland. It is a 'gold village' reconstructed by a stream in the forests, and combines the history of over a century of goldwashing in the province with the opportunity to pan for gold yourself under expert guidance. Self-catering accommodation is available. *Rovaniemi 230km/142mi.*

Tornio/Torneå N5

(pop. 22,000) At the northernmost end of the Gulf of Bothnia, Tornio is a border town, facing Sweden's Haparanda (p. 122) across the River Tornio. Its port is 10km/6mi from the town. Quite a few older buildings remain in this peaceful provincial town which has been a trading centre since the 14th century; they include the wooden church (1686). The Tornio Valley Museum is worth visiting, especially if you are planning to travel north through the landscape fed by this border

Ruskaa, *near Utsjoki*

river with Sweden. *Helsinki 760km/ 472mi.*

Utsjoki   B9

This thinly scattered community, close to the northern border with Norway, is a major Same centre near the confluence of the Utsjoki and Tenojoki rivers (famous salmon fishing). A road now follows the border south along the Tenojoki and Inarijoki rivers through very remote wilderness country to Angeli. The church (1860) is one of the few in Lappi to have survived World War II. There is good fishing in the rivers and hiking across tundra and through forests of dwarf birch. *Rovaniemi 467km/289mi.*

ICELAND

Far flung out to sea, Iceland straddles the Mid-Atlantic Ridge, a 20,000km/ 12,000mi section of submarine mountain ranges created by the upheavals of the earth's crust many millions of years ago. As the continents of America and Europe slowly creep further apart, the Atlantic Ocean floor widens at the rate of about 2½cm/1in a year and, along with it, Iceland widens too. The oldest rocks yet dated are only about 16 million years old. It is a young land, still in the making, and there are few other places where you are more aware of nature's immutable forces.

Of her total area of 103,300sq km/39,750sq mi, only about a quarter is habitable, mostly in the coastal areas and in some of the broad valleys running down to the coast from the highlands. The rest is made up of glaciers, volcanoes and their attendant expanses of lava, other non-volcanic mountains, hot springs, sand and gravel deserts and large stretches of stony wilderness. All this is liberally laced with waterways ranging from rushing rivers and chattering streams to numerous lakes.

Glaciers cover 11½ per cent of the country, the largest of them, Vatnajökull, is a sprawling white mass of 8400sq km/3240sq mi, as big as all the glaciers of continental Europe put together. In thickness, it reaches an impressive 1000m/3280ft, and one of its outlets extends to about 120m/400ft below sea level. In the south of this massif is Iceland's highest point, Öraefajökull (2119m/6950ft). Four other mighty glaciers are Langjökull and Hofsjökull in the Central Highlands, Mýrdalsjökull in the south, and Drangajökull in the north west. There are numerous smaller ones too, so that you are rarely without an ice cap on or just over the horizon.

Science fiction landscapes form the backdrop to a deep-rooted Icelandic culture which flourished in the farms and small communities from early medieval times and survives in the sagas and other early Icelandic literature, and in the Althing (Parliament), one of the world's oldest democratic legislative bodies.

Many of the forces of nature have been harnessed to provide power and heating for the needs of modern society and to inject a much-needed diversification into the national economy which, until recent years, was based almost entirely on fishing and its by-products. Today, Iceland has energy for sale and an increasing number of foreign investors are interested in purchasing this precious commodity. Hopefully this may help to alleviate the country's (pop. 226,724) massive rate of inflation which necessitates the review of salaries and foreign exchange rates several times a year.

A few years ago, a road was built along the south-east coast at the foot of Vatnajökull massif and this remarkable engineering feat completed the route round the whole of Iceland. The principal sights are listed in the following sections on North and South Iceland, but it is strongly recommended, if you have the time, to take one of the many organized tours into the uninhabited interior. These usually take the form of camping trips with tents and all meals provided. Sturdy vehicles are used over the extremely rough tracks

that penetrate landscapes of the utmost wild magnificence. If you have a special interest in birds, plants or geology you will be particularly well served.

Akureyri and the North   C9

(pop. 12,500)   The principal town of northern Iceland, Akureyri is a pleasant unpretentious place with a fine situation on the mountainous shoreline of Eyjafjördur, about 60km/37mi from the open sea. Its most dominant building is the church completed in 1940 and reached by 112 steps from the town centre. There are several museums of local interest and also Iceland's best botanical gardens containing over 2000 species and varieties from all over the world. This quiet little town periodically bursts into life when a cruise ship calls or summer coachloads of visitors arrive. A short drive away on the slopes of Hlidarfjall is Iceland's main ski hotel.

About 100km/62mi east is the most famous area in northern Iceland: **Mývatn**, a lake with such an extraordinary geological setting and richness of bird life (perhaps the world's largest concentration of breeding duck) that it acts as a magnet for ornithologists and geologists the world over. The lake covers 38sq km/15sq mi and lies at the heart of a once very active volcanic area on a plateau about 300m/1000ft high. There is a road all the way round it. A curious feature is the little church at Reykjahlid, which, though virtually surrounded by lava, stands untouched in a small clearing. Near Reykjahlid, a bleak lava field is rent by a profound fissure and here there are caves containing the hot water bathing pools of Stóragjá and Grjótagjá. Even stranger is the lava field of Dimmuborgir (black castles), a tormented landscape created about 2000 years ago on the east shore of the lake; take care not to get lost. A few miles

Akureyri

east of Reykjahlid are the pale, parched hills of Námaskard and, on the plain below, bubbling pits of blue, grey or red mud, clear pools, all steaming and hissing incessantly amid warning notices in several languages telling you to be very wary of where you tread.

Further east you reach the canyon of the glacial river Jökulsá á Fjöllum thundering down from distant Vatnajökull towards the north coast; on the way it forms Europe's mightiest waterfall, **Dettifoss**. Such is the force of water that the canyon is being lengthened at the rate of 1m/3ft per year. The sight and sound are staggering. A little to the north is **Ásbyrgi National Park**, partly composed of the former bed of the canyon before the river changed course; the lushness and variety of the vegetation is quite startling, as is the fantastic geological architecture of Hjódaklettar, a section of the park where cliffs and towers of rock have been torn and twisted by forces of unimaginable power. Nearby on this northern coast at **Tjörnes** are the fascinating crumbling cliffs composed of fossilized molluscs and plants ranging in age from several thousand to several million years. These cliffs include evidence of creatures found only in the

Pacific. To the south is the attractively placed little fishing town of **Húsavík** with views out to the island of **Grímsey**. This northernmost fragment of Iceland, which actually straddles the Arctic Circle, can be visited by air or boat from Akureyri.

The rugged Austfirdir (eastern fjords) lie a little over 300km/188mi east of Akureyri. The small but important port of **Seydisfjördur** is the main centre and, a little inland, **Egilsstadir**, by the long lake of Lagarfljót, is well placed for exploring the area. The lake is fed by the icy waters flowing down from Vatnajökull and is said to harbour a monster. At **Hallormsstadur**, on its eastern shore, one of Iceland's few forests (and its largest) is the result of experimental re-afforestation earlier this century.

The north-west coast of Iceland is made up of the great clawlike peninsula of Vestfirdir (western fjords), a mainly wild region of deep fjords, sheer cliffs and basalt rock. **Isafjördur** (pop. 3000) is the main community, depending mainly on fishing and the fish-processing industries. From here the scheduled boat service, calling at small communities all around the deeply indented fjord system, also provides a memorable full-day excursion.

Reykjavík
and the South   H4

(pop. 85,000) Reykjavík, the Icelandic capital, means 'smoke bay': a combination of the many thermal springs in the area and the fine natural harbour; it is actually a completely smokeless city. It developed from a small community at the turn of the century and even now gives the impression of a toy town, with its neat streets of red, blue, green and yellow houses, many built of corrugated iron, bordered by lava fields, pastures and the sea, and overlooked by Esja mountain (909m/2982ft). From the observation platform at the top of Hallgríms church tower you get a good idea of the layout. In front of the church is the imposing statue of Leifur Eiríksson who discovered North America.

The city centre is near the harbour, with the greystone Parliament (Althing, 1881) next to the slightly older little cathedral on Austurvöllur square, near the main post office. This district is separated from the newer business and shopping areas by Laekjargata, at the northern end of which is the grassy mound of Arnarhóll, sheltering the cosy building that houses the offices of the President and Prime Minister, and the statue of Ingólfur Arnarson, Iceland's first settler. Near here, on Laekjartorg, there is a small tourist information tower. Arnarhóll is also the focal point for national celebrations. The southern end of Laekjargata brings you to Tjörnin, a large and delightfully rural pond on which there is always a varied collection of ducks and seabirds waiting to be fed. South of this is the National Museum and Art Gallery, the university, ultramodern Nordic House (cultural exhibitions) and the Árni Magnusson Manuscript Museum harbouring a unique collection of ancient manuscripts, including some of the ancient sagas. Nearby are the expanses of domestic Reykjavik Airport; the international airport is at Keflavik (50km/31mi W).

The most charming of Reykjavík's museums is Árbaer Folk Museum on the eastern outskirts, comprising a collection of rare old buildings. Otherwise there are several worthwhile galleries for those interested in art and sculpture, among them Kjarvalsstadir, Ásgrimur Jónsson Art Gallery, Einar Jónsson gallery and the sculptures of Ásmundur Sveinsson. A summer show in English, called 'Light Nights', gives a pleasant introduction to Icelandic traditional tales and folk songs.

There are organized sightseeing tours of the city and many half- and full-day excursions in summer into the countryside of south-west Iceland where many of the main sights are concentrated. Several of them are usually combined in one tour.

To the east of Reykjavik is **Thingvellir** (50km/31mi) where, in a setting of great drama, the Icelandic national assembly met against a backdrop of volcanic cliffs from about 930. **Laugarvatn** (75km/46mi E) is a popular lake in a wild setting, with a riding centre. **Gullfoss** (122km/76mi E) is one of Europe's greatest waterfalls and a spectacular sight. **Geysir** (116km/72mi E) has given its name to hot springs and water heaters all over the world; the original Great Geysir tends to be lazy these days, but nearby Strokkur spews out a mighty water spout at intervals of a few minutes. The surrounding area is a bubbling cauldron of mud of many colours and crystal clear pools. At **Skálholt** (92km/57mi E) is the Christian heart of the country on which a church has stood for nine centuries; the present exquisitely simple building dates from only 1963. Finally there is **Hveragerdi** (46km/28mi SE) famous for the hot springs that feed its greenhouses and now there is also a well-equipped Nature Cure Sanatorium.

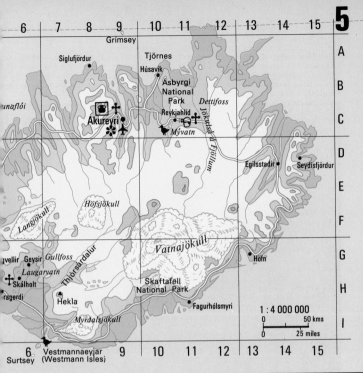

The following destinations are further afield and preferably require at least two days. The **Snaefellsnes** peninsula, about 250km/155mi north of Reykjavik, points a massive finger out into the Atlantic and has very strong associations with both the fact and fiction of the sagas, especially Laxdaela saga and Eyrbyggia saga. It was also from this coast, just east of the busy little fishing port of **Stykkishólmur**, that Eirikur Raudi (Eric the Red), outlawed for some crimes, set sail and discovered Greenland. Snaefellsnes is topped by the ice cap of Snaefellsjökull from whose central crater began Jules Verne's 19th-century novel *Journey to the Centre of the Earth*. Modern ascents of this distinctive mountain (1446m/4730ft) can begin near the fishing village of **Arnarstapi**, but you should have a guide. The peninsula, incidentally, has some of the most varied and colourful geological formations in the country.

About 135km/84mi south east of Reykjavik is **Thjórsárdalur**, Iceland's longest river valley, overlooked by one of its most famous and restless landmarks, volcanic **Hekla** (1491m/4891ft) which has erupted several times in recent years. It dominates a wild, sparsely inhabited area which, in saga times, prior to a major eruption in 1104, was fertile farmland. Dating from that period is the farm of **Stöng**, now restored and well worth visiting for itself and its setting.

One of the most exciting trips of all is via the remarkable and recently completed road along the south-east coast to **Höfn** (484km/301mi) which is becoming something of a tourist centre. The road passes by **Skaftafell National Park**, a magnificent area at the southern fringes of the Vatnajökull massif, beneath Öraefajökull. The contrasts between vivid green vegetation, deserts of black sand, white glaciers and the waters streaming from them to the sea are unforgettable. Skaftafell can be visited on a day excursion from Höfn, from which there are also glacier trips on to outlying areas of Vatnajökull. From Höfn you can also explore Austfirdir (eastern fjords; p. 69).

Day trips and longer stays are arranged from Reykjavik to the **Westmann Isles** (Vestmannaeyjar) off the south coast, where the mighty eruption of Helgafjell

(Holy Mountain) in 1973 partially buried the little town of **Heimaey** and caused the urgent evacuation of the entire population of about 5300. Its continuing rebuilding is a heart-warming example of grit and a visit to this unusual place, literally risen from the ashes, makes a lasting impression. The islands are also known for their egg-collectors who swing from ledge to ledge down vertical cliffs. The seabird life is rich indeed. A short distance from the Westmann Isles is **Surtsey** another volcanic product, born in 1963. Access is limited to scientists.

Gullfoss waterfall

Mount Hekla

Strokkur

(Background) Black castles near Mývatn

NORWAY

Scenically, Norway is one of the most dramatic countries in the world. Surrounded on three sides by sea, its coastline of about 3300km/2100mi stretches to 26,400km/16,400mi – or over half the circumference of the earth – when you include the astonishing complexity of its indentations and larger islands. Its land frontiers consist of 1619km/1005mi shared with Sweden, 716km/444mi with Finland, and 196km/122mi with the Soviet Union. It is largely composed of high plateaus intersected in the south east by deep valleys and in the west by labyrinthine fjords. More than half its surface is over 600m/2000ft high, much of it of a desolate magnificence; the highest point, Glittertinden, in the Jotunheim range, is 2472m/8110ft. All this, contained within an area of 320,000sq km/123,500sq mi, is shared by a population of little over 4 million.

Some of Scandinavian man's earliest traces (notably rock carvings) are in Norway. In the Middle Ages, following the colonizing escapades of the Norwegian Vikings, Norway's territory was more than twice its present size, and outposts included Iceland, Greenland and fragments of Britain. Many of the most interesting sights have their origins in those times. Later, many overseas possessions were ceded to Denmark and, until independence was declared in 1905, Norway's political fortunes were closely, and often uncomfortably, linked first with Denmark and, in the 19th century, with Sweden.

Most of the population, however, had to struggle so hard for a livelihood in remote valleys and fjords, that what went on beyond their particular mountain was of academic importance. Many excellent open-air museums illustrate this past way of life. It could take weeks to reach the nearest town, involving arduous journeys by horse and/or boat. Out of such journeys came the first simple staging posts for rest and worship; some of Norway's most famous hotels and interesting churches developed from these humble origins. Remoteness bred a high degree of self-sufficiency and gave rise to many of the skills and art forms which survive today; the timber-built stave churches, for example, of which about 25 survive from the 12th or 13th century, are unique to Norway. The beautiful rustic art of rose painting, which reached its peak in the late 18th and early 19th centuries and embellishes interiors and furniture in several regions, has many local variations. The

rose, incidentally, is only one motif of this art form which also includes geometric patterns, figures and even landscapes. Folk music, ballads and dancing have their roots in early medieval times, and trolls, battles and other heroic deeds are recurrent themes. Later influences came from mercenaries returning from the war in Poland around 1600, and the 'polsdans' evolved into a special Norse folk dance – a hybrid of old and new with many regional variations.

In due course, tracks became lanes and, by dint of remarkable engineering feats, main roads and railways bored through apparently impenetrable terrain. Almost any journey in Norway would qualify as scenic elsewhere, and many are utterly breathtaking. Even for those without a car, the complex network of air, bus, rail, ferry and hydrofoil services operating (mostly) like clockwork, make it possible to visit the remotest areas with ease, though not necessarily with speed. Walkers will find unparalleled opportunities for expending their energy, especially by taking advantage of the unique facilities of the Norwegian Mountain Touring Club (p. 23). Note that the distances quoted in the gazetteer apply to roads and, when planning your journey, it is important to allow for any ferry crossings involved, especially in the fjord areas.

EASTERN NORWAY

The southern part of Norway falls naturally into two regions and this section deals with the long, deep eastern valleys that drop down from the central plateaus to the Skagerrak and Oslofjord. One of the most northerly valleys, Gudbrandsdalen, provides the main link between Oslo and Trondheim and thence northern Norway. Several others, notably Hallingdal and

Setesdal, offer throughways to the western fjords of our next section.

These valleys harbour Norway's most famous winter sports resorts, and reach to the fringes of some of its most magnificent hiking country – Hardangervidda, Jotunheimen, Dovrefjell. The region also includes two major inland waterway systems: Mjøsa, the country's largest lake, and the Telemark Canal probing deep into the mountains. It was in Telemark and in Hallingdal that the art of rose painting achieved its finest expression and in these areas, too, that some of the best examples of early stave churches survive. Telemark is also known as the home of modern skiing.

Despite the ravages of fire and battle, much attractive rural and urban architecture survives. There are interesting contrasts between the weathered old homesteads of the mountain valleys or coastal fishing villages, and the bright white-painted houses which proliferated along the coast when white paint (more expensive than the rest) became a status symbol and mark of affluence. These coastal waters, incidentally, are said to be the warmest north of the Mediterranean. The imprint of the Danish-Norwegian king, Christian IV, is apparent, too, in townships ranging from Oslo to Røros, based on the Renaissance grid plan principle which reduced the hazard of fire.

Dombås   E8

(pop. 1200) This is a winter sports resort and centre for the Dovrefjell region. It stands at the junction of roads for Oslo, Trondheim and Ålesund. At **Dovre** (13km/8mi S), Tofte farm illustrates Viking Age traditions. From **Fokstua** (10km/6mi N) there are splendid views of Snøhetta (2286m/7500ft) and access to Fokstumyra moors, famous for their flora and fauna. *Oslo 345km/214mi.*

Fagernes   H8

(pop. 2500) This is the small urban hub of the Valdres valley as it bores its way north west towards the mountain massif of Jotunheimen. It is also the terminus of the Valdres railway, which starts out from Oslo. Valdres Folk Museum has a good collection of ancient timber buildings and there are stave churches to be seen in or near the valley, such as those of **Reinli** and **Hedalen** (respectively about 25km/15mi and 60km/37mi SE) and **Lomen** (about 30km/18mi NW). From mountain hotels there are fine views of Jotunheimen, but the setting and the views become increasingly stunning as you climb north up the valley from Fagernes to **Beitostølen** (40km/25mi), a popu-

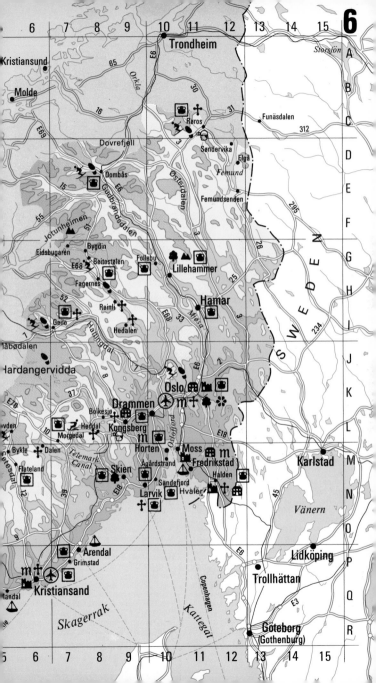

Jotunheimen mountains

lar winter sports centre with special facilities for the handicapped, and **Bygdin** (53km/33mi) at the foot of Jotunheimen massif. Opportunities for hiking, climbing and fishing in the area are legion. From Bygdin, there is a high-altitude motorboat route westwards along Bygdin lake to **Eidsbugaren**. From Bygdin, too, begins the superb Jotunheimen Road running east across the mountain plateau to **Skåbu** (52km/32mi), a truly scenic thoroughfare leading eventually to Gudbrandsdalen. Northwards from Bygdin, the main road reaches its highest point at Valdresflya (8km/5mi). *Bergen 348km/215mi.*

Fredrikstad   N11
(pop. 30,000) One of Norway's showplaces is the old fortress town facing the newer districts of Fredrikstad across the River Glomma. Within its walls are the beautifully preserved cobbled streets, houses, barracks, *etc*, of the fortified town founded and developed in the 17th and 18th centuries, in which today many

craftsmen and designers have made their studios where you can watch them at work. Outside the walls is a pinnacle topped by the slightly earlier Kongsten Fort, popular for outings and festivals. West of Fredrikstad is the famous sailing centre of **Hankø** and south is the resort area of the **Hvaler islands**. To the east the countryside is dotted with prehistoric remains, many of which can be visited by taking the Road of the Ancients (highway 110) for 17km/10mi towards Skjeberg. Sights include burial mounds, Bronze Age rock carvings (**Begby**, **Hornes** and **Solberg**) and the impressive stone circles of the 2000-year-old burial grounds at **Hunn**. *Oslo 88km/54mi.*

Geilo   I7
(pop. 2000) Scandinavia's best-known ski resort is spread beside one of a series of small lakes in a shallow valley between the plateaus of Hardangervidda and Hallingskarvet. It has three chairlifts, several drag lifts, 100km/62mi of marked ski trails and accommodation of all grades. In

Hardangervidda

summer, it offers fine walking, fishing and riding, and good excursions for motorists. **Hol** Museum (11km/7mi NE) illustrates a farm complex from the 18th century; only 1km/½mi further is 13th-century Hol Church. *Oslo 250km/155mi.*

Halden N12
(pop. 27,000) This town is on the River Tista flowing into Iddefjord which forms the border between Norway and Sweden. Today bustling with timber and other industries, it was for long a strategic outpost against Sweden and is dominated by the great fortress of Fredriksten, begun in 1661, on the crags above the town. Its ramparts, towers and underground passages are fascinating to visit, with interesting museums and superb views. Halden's older buildings are in gracious Empire style, including Immanuel Church, and Fredrikshalds Theatre has a Baroque stage, unique in Norway. Near the town is 18th-century Rød Manor and, 9km/5mi W, the impressive **Svinesund Bridge**, over Iddefjord to Sweden, soars high above the regular excursion boats that go to Strömstad in Sweden. *Oslo 119km/74mi.*

Hamar H11
(pop. 16,000) Hamar is a pleasant small town beside Mjøsa, Norway's largest lake. By the ruins of its 12th-century cathedral is the Hedemark Museum with an open-air folk collection, but a more famous attraction is the Railway Museum with its ancient rolling stock still in operation. Also notable is the *Skibladner*, launched in 1856 and possibly the world's oldest paddle boat still functioning. It plies a regular route across Mjøsa's waters between Eidsvoll, Hamar, Gjøvik and Lillehammer. *Oslo 123km/76mi.*

Hardangervidda K6
This rocky mountainous plateau, covering about 7500sq km/2900sq mi at an average height of 1000–1250m/3300–4000ft, offers magnificent trekking for the experienced. It is broken up by innumerable lakes and pools and Norway's biggest herds of wild reindeer roam its lonely landscapes. To the north west, the plateau descends abruptly to the western fjords creating dramatic ravines, as can be seen from the Geilo-Voss/Bergen road that plunges into the narrow, tortuous valley of **Måbødalen** to Eidfjord, an arm of Hardangerfjord. At the head of this valley, the thunderous waterfall of **Vøringfoss** (visible from the grounds of a hotel) is spectacular.

Horten M10
(pop. 14,000) The interesting Naval Museum of Karl Johansvern reflects Horten's original status as Norway's premier naval base (now Bergen). The town is linked by regular ferry to Moss across Oslofjord. In Borre Nature Park (3km/2mi S) 29 great burial mounds include those of the Ynglinge kings and queens said to be descended from Odin himself. **Ågårdstrand** (10km/6mi S) is a charming place of neat wooden houses and flower-filled gardens. Its bridge was made famous by Munch's painting *Girls on the Bridge* (1899) and his humble home here is a museum. *Oslo 90km/56mi.*

Hovden L5
The beautiful valley of Setesdal penetrates deep into the heart of the mountains and, near the head of it, is the lakeside summer and winter sports centre of Hovden. A distinctive peasant culture has survived in this once remote valley, silverware being one of many traditional

Stave church, Heddal

handicrafts. **Bykle** (29km/18mi S) is a typical Setesdal village, its church decorated with folk art. Near **Flateland** (50km/31mi S) is the excellent Setesdal open-air museum of Rygnestad. *Kristiansand 219km/136mi.*

Kongsberg   L9

(pop. 19,000) The town is attractively placed on the River Lågen with one of several waterfalls tumbling through the centre. It was founded by Christian IV in 1624 after the discovery of silver in the area. The silver mines at **Saggrenda** (7km/4mi S), which at their peak employed 4500 miners, closed in 1957, but visits are arranged throughout summer, travelling by the little mining train under the guidance of an old miner. In the town is the interesting Mining Museum and, near it, Norway's modern Royal Mint. Kongsberg's large Rococo church (1761) is most impressive. It can seat 2400 and the lavish decor gives it a theatrical appearance, complete with enclosed boxes from which visiting royalty and local

dignitaries could gaze down upon the congregation. Though the interior is of wood, it has been painted to resemble marble, and the final touch is added by glittering locally-made candelabra. Lågdal Museum is a collection of old farm buildings illustrating peasant culture. A cliff near the town bears the monograms of every Norwegian king since 1623.

Kongsberg lies at a major crossroads of routes to south and west Norway. **Heddal** (46km/29mi SW) has the largest and grandest stave church in Norway (magnificent carvings), dating from the 13th century. **Bolkesjø** (27km/17mi W) is a delightful small resort set in typical Telemark forested mountain scenery. *Oslo 81km/50mi.*

Kristiansand   Q6

(pop. 61,000) One of the many towns founded (1641) by Christian IV, Kristiansand is a bustling port and capital of the south coast. There are ferries to Hirtshals and Hanstholm in Denmark. Shipping and exports are its principal activities, and there is a salty, seafaring atmosphere, not least round the fish market where live fish are sold from troughs, and in the several harbours bobbing with pleasure boats. Historically, the most interesting sights are medieval Oddernes Church (runic stone in the churchyard), Christiansholms Fort (1674) bristling with old cannon, and Vest-Agder open-air museum. There are lovely boat trips out through the skerries, and from Grovane (20km/12mi NW) an 1895 steam train, operated by the Setesdal Railway Hobby Club, chugs along 5km/3mi of track through a delightful setting.

Grimstad (48km/30mi N) has a beautiful position looking out to the skerries; it was here that Ibsen served as an apothecary's assistant when he wrote his first play, and the house where he lived is now a museum. Prettily terraced against the hillsides round its harbours, **Arendal** (67km/41mi N) is one of the popular seaside and boating centres of this coast. Another is **Mandal** (42km/26mi S), Norway's southernmost· town with a famous sandy beach (Sjøsander), 3km/2mi long. *Kristiansand–Oslo 322km/ 200mi.*

Larvik   N9

(pop. 8650) This small town on an inlet of Oslofjord has regular ferry links with Frederikshavn, Denmark. Points of interest include the church (1677), the Maritime Museum in the old Customs House and Herregården with the Larvik Museum. The surroundings have much worth seeing. To the south there is Stavern where the old naval base, built in 1750, has a number of protected buildings. In the vicinity, to the south west, is 12th-century **Tanum Church** and, to the south east, **Kaupang**, Norway's oldest known Viking trading centre, has been excavated. To the north east, towards Sandefjord, is the stone circle of **Istrehågan** and the rock carvings of **Jåberg**.

Sandefjord itself (18km/11mi NE; pop. 34,000) has long lived off the sea, its merchant and whaling fleets making it Norway's third largest shipping centre; it has ferry links with Strömstad in Sweden. The Whaling Museum is particularly interesting; others are the Maritime and Town Museums. The sandy beaches and rocky coves of this coastline make it a top resort area. *Oslo 129km/80mi.*

Lillehammer   H10

(pop. 21,000) This tourist and industrial centre is the gateway to the 200km/124mi-long Gudbrandsdal valley, the age-old route between Trondheim (and the Atlantic) and Oslo. The River Mesna tumbles

through it, dropping into Norway's largest lake, Mjøsa, with summer trips on the historic paddle boat *Skibladner* (p. 77). The collections of the Maihaugen open-air museum – the life's work of a dentist, Anders Sandvig – are among the best in Norway, with 120 buildings from Gudbrandsdal set in a leafy park. The Lillehammer Art Gallery is also excellent. The town offers many facilities for outdoor activities, including guided mountain hikes. **Aulestad**, near Follebu (18km/11mi NW), is the home of the national poet, Nobel prize winner Bjørnstjerne Bjørnson, a fervent campaigner for human rights. Now a museum, it is exactly as when he died (1910). *Oslo 185km/115mi.*

Morgedal   L7

Here traditionally is the cradle of modern skiing. Its pioneer was Sondre Norheim who introduced the simple binding which firmly attached ski to boot while still allowing the necessary freedom of movement; from this idea developed all the more intricate bindings of the modern ski. His cottage, Øvrebrø, is a museum in a beautiful situation above the village. At **Bjåland Museum** there are collections of skis and polar equipment; this is named after Olav Bjåland, a native of Morgedal who participated in some of Amundsen's polar expeditions. *Oslo 195km/121mi.*

Oslo   K10

(pop. 470,000) The Norwegian capital, clustered round the head of Oslofjord, is probably the most spacious city in the world, its metropolitan area of over 450,000sq km/173,000sq mi consisting of 75 per cent forest and farmland and 5 per cent water. Its fine deep harbour probes into the heart of the city and, from it, the great cruise ships come and go, and also the ferry services to Copenhagen and Frederikshavn in Denmark, Newcastle (UK) and Kiel (Germany). It is built on some of the world's oldest rocks and man's earliest traces are 3000-year-old rock carvings near the Seamen's School on the southern outskirts of the city. Later history is found in the ruins of 11th-century St Hallvard Church and other buildings in the Gamlebyen (old town) district, off Bispegata, east of Oslo Central Station (Oslo S). The town gained much greater importance at the end of the 13th century with the building of massive Akershus fortress which was completely destroyed by fire in 1624. Christian IV then supervised the planning of the new city to the west of the old site and renamed it Christiania. It reverted to its original name in 1905 when Norway gained her

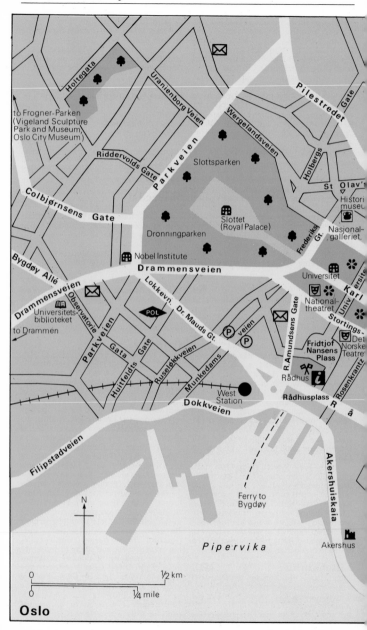

Oslo

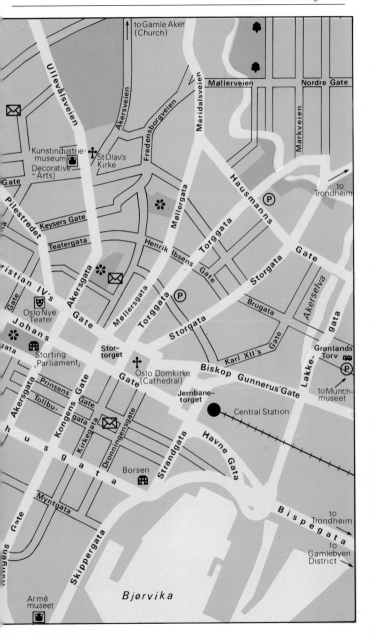

Royal Palace

Viking ship, Bygdøy

Vigeland

(Background) Holmenkollen ski jump, Oslo

independence from Sweden.

Rising above Pipervika harbour on Rådhusplass (City Hall Square) is Oslo's famous City Hall, inaugurated in 1950 for the city's 900th anniversary and lavishly decorated in the 1930s and 40s. Huge murals illustrate many aspects of contemporary Norway (Sørensen, Rolfsen, Krohg). Using the harbourside entrance, you will find the Tourist Information Office (ask for the excellent *Oslo Guide* and a copy of *Oslo This Week*). From here regular sightseeing tours (various itineraries) leave. From here, too, come and go the commuter boats to and from the peninsulas and islands of outer Oslo, the sightseeing boats, the ferry across to the headland of Bygdøy (see below), and the daily shrimp boats with their catches fresh from the sea.

Ferries, buses, subway and local trains make up the city transport. Grønlands Torv, east of Oslo Central Station, is the main bus terminal, while Oslo Central is the main railway station for all services except to the south west, which go from Oslo West (Oslo V), just west of the City Hall. From the City Hall it is only a short walk north up Roald Amundsens gate to the National Theatre and the parks that border Oslo's main thoroughfare of Karl Johans gate, with the 19th-century Royal Palace (Changing of the Guard daily at 1340) at one end and Oslo Central Station at the other. The grounds of the Palace are open to all. East of the Parliament (*Storting*), the lower end of Karl Johans gate is a pedestrian shopping precinct and, just off it, on Stortorget is Oslo Cathedral built in 1694–9 (restored, fine doors with bronze reliefs) and statue of Christian IV. A flower market flourishes on the square. Also on or just off this lively main street are the old university and Oslo's main shops.

Rising above the harbour, south of the City Hall, is the great hulk of Akershus Castle rebuilt in Renaissance style in the 17th century on the site of the medieval fortress; it houses the Defence and Resistance Museums, the latter a moving, factual memorial to World War II. If, however, you are attracted by seafaring adventures, you should head for **Bygdøy** (ferry from the City Hall). Here you will find the Viking Ships, the Kon-Tiki, Fram and Ra Museums and the Maritime Museum. The Viking Ships (*Oseberg, Gokstad* and *Tune*) are among the finest surviving. The *Fram* is the original vessel used for polar exploration by Nansen, Amundsen and Sverdrup from 1893–1912. Thor Heyerdahl's *Kon-Tiki*, the balsa raft he used for the voyage from Peru across the Pacific to Polynesia in 1947, has now been joined by his papyrus-built *Ra II* (replica of a vessel of ancient Egypt) in which his international expedition crossed the Atlantic in 1970. The Maritime Museum offers a splendid picture of seafaring Norway; including the polar exploration vessel *Gjøa* in which Amundsen was the first to negotiate the Northwest Passage. Near the Viking Ships is the Norwegian Folk Museum, a fine collection of ancient buildings including a 13th-century stave church, Lapland section and Henrik Ibsen's study.

Two other Oslo 'musts' focus on art. The Vigeland Sculpture Park and Museum in Frogner Park, north west of the centre, is dedicated to the imposing life's work of the remarkable sculptor Gustav Vigeland. His 192 sculpture groups in bronze, granite and wrought iron depict the various stages of the human cycle from birth to death. It culminates in a monolith illustrating the struggle for life and was completed in 1943, a year after his death. In the same park, 18th-century Frogner Manor contains the Oslo City Museum. North east of the centre is the Munch Museum devoted to Norway's foremost painter Edvard Munch whose often sombre but magnificent canvases reflect a childhood dominated by poverty, sickness and death. Nearby is the Natural History Museum with botanical gardens. To the north of the centre, the 12th-century church of Gamle Aker is worth seeking out. Other sights to be considered are the National Gallery and Historical Museum behind the old university.

On the heights behind the city is Hol-menkollen whose famous and huge ski jump is the scene of the annual Holmenkollen Ski Festival (March). Here is the Norwegian Ski Museum and the surroundings offer fine walks and views over the city. Another magnificent viewpoint is Tryvannstårnet observation tower at **Voksenkollen**. Both places can be reached by suburban train from the National Theatre, and a short walk. Northwards the mountains of the Nordmarka extend over an enormous area (splendid summer walking and winter skiing), dropping down to the west into the beautiful lake of Tyrifjord.

Oslo night life is fairly sedate and rather expensive, but there are plenty of good restaurants.

Røros   C11
(pop. 2000) Close by the Swedish border, this 17th-century mining town set on a high plateau has the dual attraction of its fine surroundings and an unusual industrial history. The town sprang up when copper working began in 1644 (discontinued in 1977), and much has been carefully preserved from those early days when Røros was linked by the Copper Way to the mining town of Falun in Sweden (p. 108), a way taken by many thousands in search of work or apprenticeships. Narrow streets, miners' cottages with turf roofs and blackened timbers, and more affluent houses in pastel tones can be seen. Conducted tours of the Christianus Quintus mine (8km/5mi) and the collections of the Copper Mine Museum, in the former administration building of Hyttstuggu, graphically illustrate mining conditions and the development of the town, which has provided the setting for many films as well as for the novels of Johan Falkberget (died 1967). The stone church dates from 1784. There are many marked hiking and skiing trails in the surroundings. *Oslo 401km/249mi.*

Skien   N9
(pop. 47,000) This industrial town was the birthplace of Henrik Ibsen. The small house to which the family moved in times of poverty, at Venstøp farm (5km/3mi NW), and the Ibsen house (Snipetorp) in the town centre can be visited; there is also a fine Ibsen collection in the Telemark County Museum in Søndre Brekke Park which also features many old houses from the region. From Skien, the **Telemark Canal**, built in 1892, penetrates the mountainous heart of the county to **Dalen** (130km/80mi W); it provides a memorable $9\frac{1}{2}$-hour journey by regular passenger boat through many locks. *Oslo 139km/86mi.*

WESTERN FJORDS

This section covers the islands, fjords and communities of the west coast, an exception being Voss which lies in the valleys between Hardangerfjord and Sognefjord. It includes the ancient city of Bergen and the oil boom town of Stavanger. The sounds, bays, inlets and fjords of this coast offer some of the most breathtaking scenery anywhere in the world. Here rugged nature is at its most extravagant. Mountains rise sheer to great heights from the labyrinth of sea arms that probe far into the inland plateaus, sometimes close to the foot of great glaciers, among them Norway's largest, Jostedalsbreen. Yet, often the ruggedness is softened by the visible presence of man, and in particular by the hundreds of thousands of fruit trees that add soft mists of blossom in spring.

Villages and small towns cling to the edge of the fjords. The largest are closest to the sea, their quaysides lively with colourful, workmanlike activity drawn from the comings and goings of fishing and cargo vessels. Folk art and traditions are still active. Rose painting, originally imported from the eastern valleys, has developed in different styles, notably in the Hardangerfjord area. This area was also the original home of the *Hardingfele* (Hardanger fiddle) with its eight strings and haunting tones, which succeeded the bagpipes in the 16th century and has become a national instrument. Traditional weddings still occur, especially around midsummer at Voss. Throughout summer, the Fana folklore programme, near Bergen, gives a fine introduction to the region's past peasant culture.

An intensive network of passenger boat, ferry and hydrofoil services reaches scores of communities and, in turn, links with road or rail services with an impressive and almost invariable clockwork precision. Though organized excursions are arranged from main holiday centres, almost any journey on the public transport system qualifies as scenic sightseeing of a high order.

Ålesund   D5

(pop. 35,000) Built on three islands, this is a major fishing port and commercial centre, its quays bustling with the colourful workmanlike activities of fishing and cargo vessels, as well as the daily visits from the coastal service. From the top of Aksla, rising almost straight out of the town, there are magnificent views and, in the park at its feet, a statue to Gange Rolf, or Rollo, one of the colourful saga figures from this area, who became feudal lord of

Normandy and was ancestor of no less than William the Conqueror. The statue was a gift from the French town of Rouen. The Sunnmøre Museum (boats from the 7th century) and the Aquarium are interesting local sights. *Bergen 379km/235mi.*

Bergen   K3

(pop. 212,000) The approach to Bergen by sea is one of the most attractive in Europe. The city is ringed by steep mountains and the centre spreads out from the harbour in an architectural medley ranging from the medieval to the modern. Passenger ferries from Newcastle, Amsterdam and Cuxhaven, and the coastal vessels that leave almost daily for north Norway, berth on the north side of the harbour near Bergenhus fortress with 13th-century King Haakon's Hall and 16th-century Rosenkrantz Tower. Between here and the eastern head of the harbour is the imposing line of gabled houses from Hanseatic times. To the south side of the harbour come the hydrofoils and regular boats linking Bergen with many parts of the western fjords. Nearby, on the western headland is Nordnes parken and the Aquarium, northern Europe's largest and most modern. And at the head of the harbour is Torget where the daily open-air market of fish, fruit, vegetables, flowers and souvenirs bustles with activity all year round from 0830–1500. The fish stalls and troughs of live fish are special Bergen features.

The city was founded in 1070 by the Viking king Olav Kyrre and developed in the Middle Ages to become the capital of Norway and the largest port and trade centre of Scandinavia, a hub of Hanseatic power and wealth. Despite fires and other disasters, much still remains from those times. The Tourist Information Office on Torgalmenning, near the market, issues an excellent annual *Bergen Guide* (free)

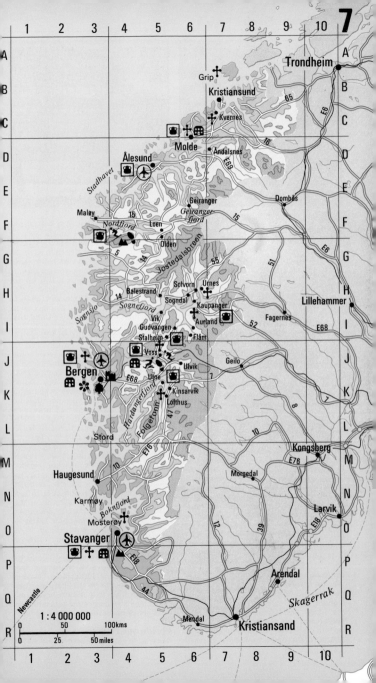

Ålesund

Bergen harbourside

detailing what's on, when and where, and it is also from here that many sightseeing excursions leave. If you prefer independent exploration, there is a 48-hour tourist ticket giving unlimited travel on public transport within the city.

Bergen's top attraction is undoubtedly Bryggen, the Hanseatic district on the north side of the harbour, where a row of ancient wooden houses with their high-pointed gables provides the frontage for a network of narrow alleys leading back into the courtyards, workshops and living quarters in which the employees of the Hansa merchants lived a virtually cloistered existence. Today it is an area of small workshops and restaurants where arts and crafts are still very much alive. In 1955, a section of Bryggen was destroyed by fire, but it has been partly reconstructed into a top-class hotel whose façade conforms in every detail with those of its ancient neighbours. Close to it is the new Bryggen Museum, displaying finds from excavations following the fire. Further east along the waterfront, one of the old houses is the Hanseatic Museum, its creaking stairs and original furnishings giving an excellent picture of the merchants' life style. Also in this part of town, behind Bryggen, is Maria Kirken (St Mary's Church), restored in the 19th century almost exactly to its original 12th-century condition (note the beautiful portals and superb 15th-century altar reredos).

If you follow Øvregaten eastwards from the church, you will soon come to the funicular station for Mount Fløien. Narrow alleys and steps wind and twist between the delightful old wooden houses stacked up the steep hillside of this district, well worth some footwork before you board the funicular. This whisks you up in a few minutes to Fløien (320m/1050ft) and a stunning aerial view

over the whole sprawl of the city. A network of marked paths provides plenty of opportunity for further exercise.

Returning to the Tourist Information centre in Torgalmenning, you are within a short walk of several cultural sights in the centre and south of the town. The Museum of Arts and Crafts and the Fisheries Museum (excellent displays illustrating the development of fishing over the centuries) are only a brief stroll from the small lake of Lille Lungegårdsvann on whose south side are the Municipal Art Gallery, the Stenersen's Collection, and the Rasmus Meyer Collection (including paintings by Munch) where piano recitals are held on summer afternoons. Across Lars Milles gate from here is the ultra-modern Grieg Hall, a main hub of Bergen's cultural life. A few blocks to the south is the complex housing the Historical, Maritime and Natural History Museums by the Botanical Gardens.

Within a few minutes drive of the city are three major attractions: Gamle Bergen (Old Bergen) open-air museum, a collection of 18th- and 19th-century houses and shops; Fantoft stave church from late Viking times; and Trollhaugen, Edvard Grieg's home, preserved with all its Victoriana. Another 'must' in the environs is the cable-car trip up mount Ulriken for more breathtaking views.

Highly popular is Fana Folklore, arranged several times weekly in summer and consisting of an evening out in the Fana countryside with traditional food and entertainment. The principal event in Bergen's calendar is the Bergen International Festival (late May to early June) featuring all aspects of the arts with top-class performances. *Oslo 495km/307mi.*

Geirangerfjord   E6

This is arguably the most scenic of

Geirangerfjord

Norway's many stunning fjords. It is regularly visited by cruise ships for the awesome spectacle of the mountains which drop in sheer rock cliffs to the fjord waters, their façades streaming with waterfalls with names like the Seven Sisters, the Suitor and the Bridal Veil. The resort of **Geiranger** has good tourist facilities and acts as the starting point for magnificent tours north to Romsdalsfjord (see Molde) and south to Nordfjord (p. 89). From the summit of Dalsnibba (1496m/4908ft), accessible by road, the views to the fjord and surrounding peaks are breathtaking. *Bergen 397km/246mi.*

Hardangerfjord   K5

This great fjord system south of Bergen has good road and rail links (from Granvin via Voss) to Bergen and Oslo, as well as year-round road connections via Telemark to eastern Norway and Oslo, and through Setesdal to Kristiansand and southern Norway. Its folklore is rich (this is the original home of the Norwegians' national instrument, the Hardanger fiddle) and colourful children's weddings are a feature of the summer programme. Orchards are one of the region's assets – about 250,000 fruit trees in all, creating magnificent mists of blossom in May. These fruit trees were brought in medieval times by Cistercian monks. To the east rises the grandeur of Hardangervidda (p. 77) while the white shoulders of Folgefonn glacier glint above Sørfjord, a southern arm of the fjord system.

Several ferries link many of the com-

Nordfjord

Aurlandsfjord

munities across the waters. **Lofthus** on Sørfjord is a delightful resort in the heart of a major fruit-growing area; it was a favourite spot of Edvard Grieg and you can see the hut in which he composed in the garden of the splendid Hotel Ullensvang. The local church dates from the 13th century. **Kinsarvik** and **Utne**, on opposite sides of the mouth of Sørfjord, are both pleasant, the latter featuring the Hardanger Folk Museum. Agatunet, a few miles south along Sørfjord, is a particularly well-preserved traditional farm complex (30–40 buildings), now a museum. **Ulvik**, on one of the innermost tributary fjords of the system, is another pleasant summer resort set in orchard and farm country. *Kinsarvik–Bergen 129km/ 80mi.*

Kristiansund   B7

(pop. 18,500) This major fishing port, built on three islands and linked by two modern bridges, is a colourful lively place, its long quays bustling with seafaring activities. It was almost entirely rebuilt following destruction by the Germans in 1940. Kristiansund is a port of call on the daily coastal service from Bergen and is linked by a beautiful road through the rugged Sunndal valley to the resort of Oppdal (164km/102mi SE) on the main rail and road routes from Oslo to Trondheim. A recommended excursion is to **Grip island**, about 3 hours north west by boat, where you will find a haunting solitude in a deserted fishing village (stave church) looking out to great seascapes. Here a community of several hundred somehow survived political and natural storms in the 17th and 18th centuries. Another excursion (south) is to **Kvernes** stave church by ferry to Bremsnes and 14km/8mi by road. *Bergen 513km/318mi.*

Molde   D6

(pop. 20,000) This smiling spacious town, famous for its roses, has a magnificent position overlooking island-studded Romsdalsfjord, backed by a panorama of 87 peaks whose full splendour is best seen from the hilltop viewpoint of Varden, 10 minutes drive from town. Molde is a port of call on the daily coastal service. It was briefly the capital of free Norway when King Haakon and the government sheltered here in 1940, at which time it was heavily bombed. The resultant modernity is striking, especially the Town Hall with its roof garden and the eye-catching church (1957, Finn Bryn) with its interior mosaics, reliefs and dazzling stained glass. Two excellent collections are the Romsdal Museum (40 buildings from the Viking Age onwards) and the Fisheries Museum (in the form of a fishing village) on the island of Hjertøya. The island is also a favourite bathing place. A popular local excursion is to **Trollkyrkja** (Troll Church), a marble grotto with subterranean waterfall; it is reached by road to Sylteseter (30km/18mi N), then 1½ hours walk. Molde's annual jazz festival in July has an international reputation.

The whole of this coast is intricately fragmented by fjords and sounds, offering many fine excursions by boat (including fishing trips) and bus. **Åndalsnes** (pop. 3000; 35km/21mi and two ferries SE) has a fabulous setting by inner Romsdalsfjord, backed by steep mountains. It is the terminus for the Rauma railway which, together with a scenically superb road, passes between the soaring mountains and thunderous waterfalls of the Romsdal valley to Gudbrandsdal (see Lillehammer, p. 79). Another famous route is Trollstigen (the Troll's Path) which twists away south from Åndalsnes, past the Stigfoss falls, eventually to Valldal and Geiranger (p. 87). *Molde–Bergen 446km/ 276mi.*

Nordfjord F4

For nearly 100km/62mi, the long narrow cleft of this fjord probes deep into the Stryn mountains and towards the foot of Jostedalsbreen, Norway's largest glacier. **Maløy** at the entrance to the fjord is served by the regular coastal service from Bergen, and bus services link the whole area with Otta on the main rail route through Gudbrandsdal. At the head of the fjord sit the resorts of **Stryn**, **Loen** and **Olden**, each with its own valley and lake, the last two beneath tongues of the glacier. There is summer skiing in the area and various routes across the glacier which should not, however, be attempted without a qualified guide. The area has experienced avalanches and rockfalls of great magnitude; one of them, in 1936, caused a tidal wave in the lake of Loen in which 74 lives and several farms were lost.

The resorts have excellent facilities and offer splendid excursions by boat, on foot or by road through very grand scenery. Highly recommended is the circuit Nordfjord–Grotli–Geiranger–Hellesylt–Nordfjord (about 200km/120mi). At Sandane, at the head of the southern tributary of Gloppenfjord, is the Nordfjord Folk Museum. *Sandane–Bergen 254km/158mi.*

Sognefjord H4

This is the first major fjord system north of Bergen, its magnificent complex of tributary fjords thrusting crooked fingers deep into the rugged interior dominated by the Jotunheimen mountains to the east and the great white glint of Jostedalsbreen (glacier) to the north. The shorelines are softened by orchards and their mists of blossom in spring. Main roads from Bergen, via Voss, and from Oslo, via Gol, plunge down to the southern shores of the fjord system and are linked by several ferries to the highways for the north. Regular services by passenger boat and hydrofoil also link the area with Bergen. One of the most stunning ferry routes in all Norway is from Gudvangen (p. 90) through Naerøyfjord which, in places, is no more than 380m/1250ft wide beneath sheer mountains soaring to over 900m/3000ft, their flanks astream with waterfalls. Not surprisingly this is a popular port of call for cruise ships, whose presence often adds to the impressiveness of the scene. Ferries link communities such as Gudvangen (Naerøyfjord), Aurland and Flåm (Aurlandsfjord), Kaupanger, Laerdal, and Årdalstangen (Årdalsfjord). **Flåm** is also the railhead for a branch line of the Oslo–Bergen railway, forming part of the highly scenic 'Norway in a Nutshell' circuit from Voss (p. 90). From **Aurland**, spectacular minor roads swoop and plunge over the mountains to Laerdal or to Hol in Hallingdal. From **Kaupanger** (stave church and Sogn folk museum) and **Sogndal**, on the north shore of the fjord system, there are fabulous routes through the Lustrafjord, Fortunsdal and Sognefjell areas. There is a particularly fine 12th-century stave church at **Urnes** on the east shore of Lustrafjord, reached by boat from Solvorn.

Further west, ferries link Vangsnes across Sognefjord with Hella, Dragsvik and **Balestrand** which has long been a famous small fjordside resort, very popular with the British and with artists. There has been an inn here for centuries, for this was a resting place in the days when it took two weeks to reach Bergen. Gradually the inn developed into the splendid hotel that dominates the waterfront. It was a favourite haunt of Kaiser Wilhelm II whose visits, accompanied by a naval flotilla, caused a certain amount of suspicion among the neutral Norwegians in World War I. Nevertheless, so taken was he with the place that Wilhelm had two monuments built in the area, one of them, to the Viking king Bele, placed on some Viking burial mounds at Balestrand. He was also here when fire broke out in the resort, and rushed over to direct firefighting operations. From Balestrand, a beautiful road leads on towards the north, first winding steeply up Gaularfjell with magnificent views. There are also boat trips up remote, lovely Fjaerlandsfjord at the foot of Jostedalsbreen (glacier). *Kaupanger–Bergen 172km/106mi.*

Stavanger O4

(pop. 88,000) Norway's main North Sea oil base and boom town is the capital of Rogaland county, poised on the threshold of the labyrinthine Ryfylke fjords that penetrate deep into this rugged coastline. From here radiates a complex network of boat and hydrofoil services, serving many fjordside communities and providing a short cut to the coast further north, including Bergen. Stavanger is an ancient city, its cathedral dating from the 12th century, when it was begun by Bishop Reinald of Winchester. British craftsmen were probably brought over for the building of this great church, originally in Anglo Norman style, though it was badly damaged by fire in 1272 and a new Gothic chancel was completed in 1300. In contrast with the broad streets of the newer town, the narrow cobbled lanes near the cathedral and harbour offer an attractive old-world atmosphere for shopping. Gamle Stavanger (Old Stavanger), above the west side of the harbour, is particularly charming with its white-painted 18th- and 19th-century houses. Other special points of interest in town are Ledål Museum, a mansion from 1800; the Stavanger Museum with its archaeological, historical, zoological and nautical collections, and the Stavanger Art Gallery.

A wide range of fjord trips include beautiful Lysefjord, with the chance to climb to the top of Prekestolen (the Pulpit), a dramatic rock cliff soaring about 550m/1800ft out of the fjord (reached by boat, bus and on foot). Fjord fishing trips are popular and Stavanger has an important International Sea Fishing Festival every August. Utstein Kloster (monastery) on the island of Mosterøy, north of Stavanger, has a beautifully preserved medieval cloister. A little outside the town, the reconstructed Iron Age farm at Ullandhaug can be visited. *Oslo 584km/362mi, Bergen 149km/92mi.*

Voss   J5

(pop. 6000) One of Norway's most popular tourist centres, Voss is situated by a lake on the famous Oslo–Bergen railway, about halfway between Sognefjord and Hardangerfjord. It is popular both as a skiing resort and an excellent centre for summer excursions into spectacular fjord country. Much of it was destroyed by bombing in 1940, so most of the buildings are new with a few notable exceptions. One of these is the fine church, stone-built in early Gothic but with a wooden oc-

tagonal tower, originally dating from about 1270. Interesting features are its upper gallery, carved Baroque rood screen, decorated Renaissance pulpit and paintings on wood panels round the chancel.

On the outskirts is Finneloftet, one of Norway's oldest secular wooden buildings (about 1250), and on a hillside above the town is Mølstertunet, a splendid open-air museum consisting of two farms, with a total of 16 buildings, graphically illustrating their development since the late Middle Ages and the tough conditions endured by the farming folk. You can see the outhouses in which the girls of the families slept – in summer in storehouses and in winter above the cattle for warmth. The museum is full of intriguing details, such as the candle marked off to calculate time as it burned down. A cable car to Hangur restaurant and a chairlift on to Hangurstoppen (817m/2680ft) give easy access to fine views and good walking.

One of Voss's greatest attractions is the variety of excursions that can be made through truly superb landscapes. 'Norway in a Nutshell' is a full-day round trip which combines bus, boat and rail travel incorporating **Gudvangen** and **Flåm** (see Sognefjord). If time is short, go at least on the first leg by road to **Stalheim** (36km/22mi NE) where the hotel perched on a mountain shelf offers phenomenal views down to Naerøyfjord. Near the hotel is a collection of traditional farm buildings and artefacts. Voss offers plenty of scope for summer activities, including fishing and windsurfing on the lake. See also Hardangerfjord. *Bergen 125km/78mi.*

Stavanger flower market

NORTH NORWAY

This section covers the immensely long narrow stretch of country from the former capital of Trondheim in the south to the Soviet border via the North Cape, and includes the island groups of the Lofotens and Vesterålen. The area is characterized by a lot of dramatic and lonely scenery, and rather few inhabitants, the ratio decreasing with the latitude!

Traces of the oldest culture (up to about 8000 BC) yet discovered in Scandinavia were found in Finnmark, the northernmost province (the Komsa culture, near Alta). The Same (Lapp) people (see also pp. 63, 118) are the oldest known inhabitants of the far north, the Norwegians gradually moving in to trade, fish and farm. A further influx of immigrants from northern Sweden and Finland, and farmers from south Norway occurred in the 18th and 19th centuries. Reindeer breeding is still an important source of livelihood for many of the 30,000 Same people, some of whom follow the herds up to the mountain plateaus in spring and back to the coast in autumn.

Many communities suffered considerable damage during World War II, either by bombing or, in the case of Finnmark, by the scorched-earth policy of the retreating German army in 1944. Most towns therefore are largely modern, though many also have a collection of historic buildings preserving the past.

Fishing continues to be the backbone of the far north's economy and the triangular drying racks are features of almost every coastal community, as are the pastel and warm tones of the houses against an often stark setting. Seafishing trips, with tackle provided, are available in many places. There is also superb angling (salmon, sea trout, migratory char, *etc*) but the strict local regulations should be checked.

Alta   E13

(pop. 7500) Traces of Norway's oldest human occupation – the Komsa culture of up to about 8000 BC – were found on nearby Komsafjell. Also significant are the rock carvings, about 2000–3000 years old, which can be seen at nearby Hjemmeluft and Amtmannsnes. The town developed from the mainly Same community of Bossekop whose important spring and autumn markets attracted Norwegians and neighbouring Swedes and Finns. Its growth was boosted by the exploitation of copper in the mid 19th century (since abandoned), and the English church at Kåfjord is from those times. Today slate quarrying is the main

industry. Boat trips on the River Alta can be arranged. It is arguably the best salmon river in the world, leased by the Dukes of Roxburghe and Westminster until 1953, and since then by Americans. *Oslo 2010km/1256mi.*

Bodø   J6

(pop. 30,000) This airy town on the regular coastal service is a main launching point for the magnificent Lofoten islands (see Svolvaer) whose jagged mountain wall can be seen to even better advantage from Rønvikfjell (restaurant), 3km/2mi from the town centre. There are also regular services to Vaerøy and Røst with their fabulous bird colonies. For instance, Røst archipelago, about 100km/62mi NW, numbers about 800 inhabitants and 4 million birds, notably huge colonies of puffin and kittiwake. Bodø's modern cathedral (1956) is strikingly light and spacious, and the Nordland County Museum presents an excellent picture of the region. Two recommended excursions are to the old trading post at **Kjerringøy** (39km/24mi and one ferry north) and **Saltstraum**, about 20km/12mi SE. The latter is a narrow channel through which a seething tide-race surges every six hours, a phenomenal sight. Shoals of fish follow in the wake of the natural bait sucked in by the ferment, making it a favourite spot for fishermen. *Oslo 1283km/797mi.*

Hammerfest   C13

(pop. 7500) Hammerfest's two claims to fame are that it is the world's northernmost town (70°40′) and was the first in Europe to get electric light (1891). Fishing and sealing are main occupations and there are huge deep-freeze installations. The modern church is splendid, its entire east wall in glowing stained glass. The town hall is the home of the Royal and Ancient Society of Polar Bears, with a

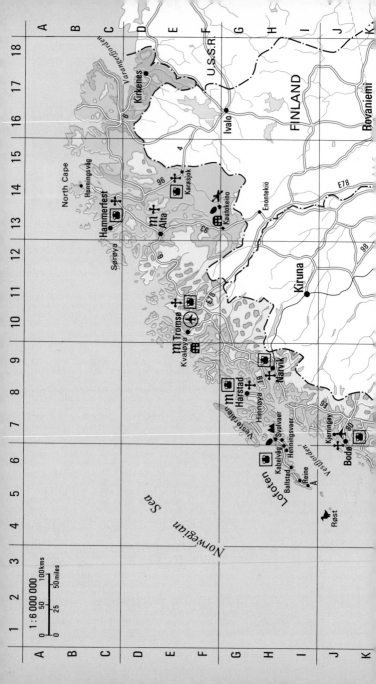

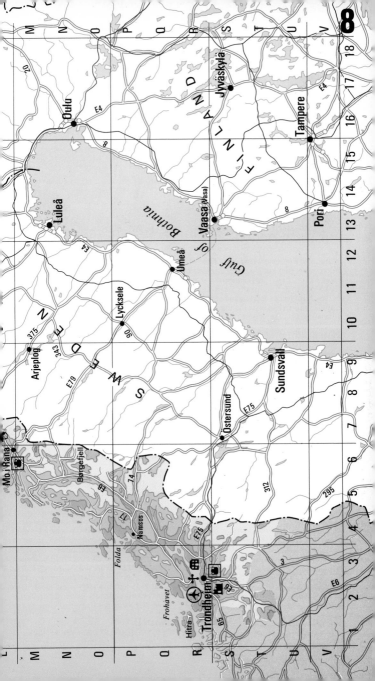

Svartisen, Mo i Rana

museum of Arctic trapping. The Meridian monument at Fuglenes commemorates the first international survey (1816–52) to determine the size and shape of the earth. Excursions include the North Cape. Hammerfest is on the regular coastal service. *Oslo 2154km/1338mi.*

Harstad   G8
(pop. 21,400) A port of call on the regular coastal service, this is a natural gateway to the Vesterålen and Lofoten island groups (see also Svolvaer) in grand surroundings. It is linked via the Tjeldsund road bridge to the mainland. At nearby Trondenes is the world's most northerly medieval church (1250), while that of Harstad is elegantly modern (1958). In the vicinity are the prehistoric rock paintings on Kjeøya islet and, at Grytøy, the Lundenes Bygdetun collection of farm buildings. The annual North Norway Music Festival is a major event around midsummer. *Oslo 1450km/900mi.*

Karasjok   E14
(pop. 1200) This village near the Finnish border is an important Same community. It has the only Lapp (Same) Museum in Norway and the world's largest library on Same subjects. The local high school has a permanent exhibition of Same handicrafts. The church (1810) is the oldest surviving in Finnmark. Excursions include river trips to a gold panning camp at **Storfossen** (60km/37mi SE). *Oslo 2276km/1414mi; Stockholm 1769km/1097mi.*

Kautokeino   G13
(pop. 1600) On a through road linking northern Norway and Finland, this is the

most important Same community in Finnmark and its largest reindeer-breeding parish. Many families still follow the herds to the coastal grazing grounds each spring, returning in the autumn. Prior to their departure, the Easter festival is the highlight of the year, an occasion for weddings in the modern church and sporting events, with the brilliant Same costumes much in evidence against the dazzling snow. There are trips by reindeer and sledding tours can be arranged in winter, while walking, canoeing and fishing are summer pursuits. The Nord Samic Institute for research into Same affairs is based in Kautokeino. The traditional craft of the silversmith is still very much alive and workshops can be visited. *Oslo 2124km/1320mi; Stockholm 1526km/946mi.*

Lofoten Islands see Svolvaer

Mo i Rana   L6
(pop. 10,000) A little south of the Arctic Circle, Mo is a modern industrial centre on Ranafjord with a huge state-owned iron foundry (guided tours available) and great factories. There are fine views from Mofjell (410m/1345ft), reached by cable car, and an interesting collection of old farm buildings, Stenneset Bygdetun (8km/5mi). To the north, the landscape is dominated by Svartisen, Norway's second largest glacier, to which excursions can be arranged; another excursion north is to the **Grønli** stalactite caves (22km/13mi). *Oslo 1035km/642mi.*

Narvik   H9
(pop. 20,000) With some of the most modern port installations anywhere,

Midnight sun, Lofoten Islands

Narvik is the world's biggest exporter of iron ore, handling the huge output from the Swedish mines of Kiruna to which it is linked by railway. This extraordinary engineering feat was completed in 1902, and stories associated with the building of the railway are part of the country's folklore. Narvik was the object of intensive fighting in World War II. There is a museum to the Battle of Narvik of 1940 and traces of heavy German fortifications can still be seen. The Peace Chapel commemorates casualties from both sides. The surroundings are imposing with snow-capped peaks, including the Sleeping Queen (said to resemble Queen Victoria on her deathbed); for breathtaking views take the cable car to Fagernesfjell. Excursions include trips to the Lofotens (see Svolvaer). *Oslo 1453km/902mi.*

North Cape B14

The towering granite cliffs soar out of the sea to over 300m/1000ft forming Europe's northernmost point (71°11′). The midnight sun is visible, subject to weather, from 14 May to 30 July. The wild, bleak plateau is reached by road across Magerøy island from the fishing port of **Honningsvåg** (pop. 4600; 34km/21mi SE) on the regular coastal route. On the plateau is the North Cape Hall with restaurant and panoramic views. Near Honningsvåg, a Same (Lapp) encampment can be visited at fixed times. *Honningsvåg–Oslo 2170km/1348mi.*

Svolvaer H7

(pop. 4500) The 'capital' of the Lofoten islands has a setting of Alpine grandeur and is linked by boat to Bodø on the regular coastal service. The famous Lofoten Wall of mountains that rise to jagged peaks, almost sheer out of the sea, stretches for some 100km/62mi facing the mainland across Vestfjord. Since the Middle Ages the area has been the scene of extraordinary activity each year (usually February to April) because of the life cycle of the *skrei*, or mature cod, which means that it travels all the way from the Barents Sea to spawn in these waters. At this time, thousands of fishermen in hundreds of vessels (and it used to be many more) converge on the area for the famous Lofotens Fisheries. The sight against the dramatic backdrop of mountains, deeply shrouded in snow, is unforgettable. The Fisheries are controlled by their own 'government' which strictly regulates the zones and tackle permissible for different types of vessel and their catches; regulations are enforced by careful policing. The harvest of the sea is hung on the innumerable triangular drying racks used for stockfish, or handled by the many, sometimes pungent, fish-processing factories.

The east coast of the islands is punctuated by pretty fishing hamlets and villages such as **Kabelvåg** (Lofoten Museum and Aquarium), **Henningsvaer**, **Ballstad**, **Reine** and **Å**, clinging to

Arctic Cathedral, Tromsø

the shore beneath the mountains. With careful planning, you can go island-hopping, using regular bus and ferry routes. If you have a taste for the simple life, you can rent a *rørbu* (simple hut formerly used by fishermen), usually in a fantastic setting, but you will need to bring all your own equipment. There are splendid walks and climbs, the latter including the famous Svolvaer 'Goat' (a rock formation in Fløyfjell above Svolvaer) with its two 'horns'; the intrepid jump from one to the other. Svolvaer and other Lofoten communities have long attracted many artists for whom there are special facilities. Among many excursions are boat trips to Trollfjord, perhaps the most awesome of all Norway's fjords. *Oslo 1387km/867mi.*

Tromsø   E10

(pop. 45,000) Situated on an island in a narrow fjord and a port of call on the regular coastal service, this northern town is known as the 'capital' of north Norway because of its extensive industrial and educational activities. Fishing, sealing, whaling, the fur trade, shipping and allied industries are its main occupations. It was from Tromsø that Roald Amundsen, commemorated by a statue, set off on some of his polar expeditions, including his last ill-fated journey by seaplane in

search of the missing Italian, Umberto Nobile. And it was from here that the king and government left for five years exile in Britain, in 1940. Here, too, is an important meteorological station and the Northern Lights Observatory.

Tromsø was one of the few northern towns that survived World War II unscathed and there are plenty of interesting old buildings, as well as the world's northernmost inn. Other points of interest are the Tromsø Museum (4km/2½mi SW), including Same and regional collections, and Tromsø Town Museum. Tromsdal Church (known as the Arctic Cathedral) is a magnificent modern building designed to harmonize with the surrounding panorama. Tromsø Cathedral itself (1861) is a large and simple wooden edifice. A cable car takes you up to Storsteinen (420m/1378ft) and fabulous views. On neighbouring Kvaløya island (road bridge) are 4000–5000-year-old rock carvings at **Skavberg** farm (27km/17mi S) and historic buildings at **Hella** (28km/17mi S). *Oslo 1714km/1063mi.*

Trondheim   R2

(pop. 135,000) Originally called Nidaros, this was once the capital of Norway and its cultural, economic and religious hub, founded by Olav Tryggvesson in 997. It is a port of call on the regular coastal service and beautifully placed astride the looping River Nid facing the fjord. The magnificent cathedral, scene of many coronations, is a national shrine and the finest Gothic edifice in northern Europe. It stands on the burial place of Olav Haraldsson (Norway's patron saint) who was slain in the battle at Stiklestad (90km/56mi N) in 1030, while seeking to complete the Christianization of Norway. The story of the battle is enacted each year at the end of July. Building of the cathedral began in the early 12th century and continued until the 14th. English medieval craftsmen were employed and there are strong similarities to some English cathedrals, especially Lincoln. After many ravages and plunderings, the cathedral was restored in 1869 (and subsequently) and is a truly impressive shrine in which soft grey-green soapstone contrasts with shimmering stained glass, the latter the life's work of Gabriel Kielland. There are several sculptures by Gustav Vigeland. Next to the cathedral is the 12th-century Archbishop's residence.

The town was rebuilt following a disastrous fire in 1681 and the broad streets and many houses and details date from that time. Stiftsgården (1774), the Rococo royal residence, is one of the largest timber buildings in Europe. Along the ancient wharves, rows of high-gabled warehouses, many from the 17th century and painted in rich colours, make a splendid impression. For fine general views of the town, go to Kristiansten fortress (1682) on a rocky eminence. Several major sights are a little outside the town. Ringve Manor, little changed since 1650, houses the Tordenskjöld Museum and the exceptional Museum of Music, in which many old and rare instruments can be seen and heard, each room devoted to a different period. The Trondheim Folk Museum at Sverresborg has splendid collections. Munkholmen island is a favourite excursion point where Viking executions once took place and later a monastery was built (no trace). *Oslo 545km/338mi.*

Moccasin-seller, Trondheim

SWEDEN

Sweden's vital statistics alone are enough to fire the imagination of enthusiasts of wide open spaces. About 1600km/1000mi long by 390km/240mi wide, with 6400km/4000mi of coastline, 150,000 islands and 96,000 lakes, it carries a population of little more than 8¼ million. The impact of its landscapes falls somewhere between the hugeness of Finland's horizons and the ruggedness of Norway's heights, yet it has more streamlined and sophisticated amenities than either of its neighbours. Affluence is a tangible presence in Sweden, seen in smart properties, large cars, big and numerous motor cruisers, the proliferation of sleek trailers, big – sometimes huge – and well-stocked supermarkets, and in the considerable automation of many of its services.

Sweden's fluctuating fortunes have left their stamp on the countryside which vies with Denmark especially in the number of churches, castles and manor houses that punctuate the fertile southern farmlands. These southlands are in great contrast to the fells and forests, wild river valleys and immense lakescapes elsewhere. Like their neighbours, the Swedes escape into the countryside gratefully at every opportunity and they are well equipped to make the most of it, whatever their taste in outdoor activities. Hotel voucher schemes, well-equipped self-catering accommodation, excellent campsites and transport bargains simplify holiday life at all budget levels.

Perhaps due to a sense of loss felt in the shift away from the simple priorities and culture bred by the wilderness, there is now a considerable movement to reaffirm traditions and to encourage or revive ancient crafts. Thus folk culture is still strong in many regions and enterprises devoted to *hemslöjd* (cottage industry) proliferate and range from regional organizations dedicated to maintaining high standards and researching forgotten skills to small workshops in the countryside, often set up by fugitives from city life.

For administrative purposes, Sweden is divided into 24 counties (*län*), but the names of the provinces – Dalarna, Skåne, Värmland, *etc*, – still survive.

SOUTH SWEDEN

The great blunt 'nose' of south Sweden separates the Baltic Sea from the Kattegat, nudging alongside the Danish islands so that it is not surprising that the southernmost beach-fringed province of Skåne

remained politically part of Denmark until 1658. Thus many Skåne towns were founded by that energetic Danish king Christian IV, and the rich, rolling farmlands of Skåne are dotted with prosperous farms and manors, and the castles built to defend them. Iron Age mounds and Viking Age runic stones are evidence of a much earlier appreciation of this fruitful soil.

The Danes and Swedes fought long over this desirable piece of land, but there was less contest over the province of Småland immediately to the north, characterized by rock, forests and lakes. It bred a people with a tough pioneer spirit who formed close-knit communities, and it was from this region, and from the adjacent island of Öland, that the greatest exodus of emigrants took place in the depressed conditions of the mid 19th century to exercise their pioneer spirit in the New World. The people of Småland are famous for their craftsmanship which still flourishes in workshops tucked away in the forests today. It remains, too, the leading region for the production of fine glass.

Further out in the Baltic, the island of Gotland had a brief medieval period of glory as a hub of Hanseatic power. On the west coast, long before Gothenburg was founded to become Sweden's chief window on the world, Bronze Age man imprinted his remarkable rock carvings on the rugged terrain of Bohuslän to the north. The construction of the Göta Canal in the 19th century forged a new link between west and east through Västergotland and Östergotland with their huge lakes, Vänern and Vättern, that overlap into our central region.

Dalsland Canal   C4

If you are an enthusiast of inland waterways, you will find endless possibilities in the intricate network of interlinked lakes serviced by the Dalsland Canal. The canal is 254km/157mi long and rises by means of 29 locks to a total of 66m/216ft above its starting point at **Köpmannebro** on Lake Vänern; but it is better described as a navigable lake system since only about 10km/6mi of its length is excavated canal. The locks also give access to adjoining lakes and the area is a paradise for canoeists for whom there is an informative free booklet in English. Canoes and motor cruisers can be rented. There are passenger boat services in summer from Köpmannebro to Bengtsfors, taking 6 hours. One of the most interesting places along the route is **Håverud** with its triple lock, aqueduct and canal museum. **Bengtsfors** is beautifully situated, with a local culture museum. **Ed**, on the interlinked lake, Stora Lee, to the west, is another charming centre. **Mellerud** (pop. 3600), a pleasant small country town by Lake Vänern, is a main starting point for exploring the area. *Mellerud–Gothenburg 131km/81mi.*

Göta Canal   F4

This remarkable waterway, created in the 19th century, links the cities of **Gothenburg** and **Stockholm** (and therefore the North Sea and Baltic Sea), an idyllic journey of three days by old-fashioned but quite comfortable motorships through rural south Sweden. Only about one third of the total of 518km/322mi is on artificial canals; the rest is through a chain of lakes and rivers, including Lakes Vänern and Vättern, a short stretch along the Baltic coast and the final approach to Stockholm through Lake Mälaren. The vessels are raised by means of 65 locks (to over 90m/300ft above sea level and down again) including the impressive lock staircases at **Trollhättan** (p. 106).

Göteborg/Gothenburg   H3

(pop. 500,000) Situated on the broad River Göta, this is Sweden's principal port and provides many visitors with their first glimpse of the country. It has sea links with Newcastle, Felixstowe, Amsterdam and Frederikshavn (Denmark). It was founded in 1621 by Gustavus Adolphus who called in Dutch planners; their canals are one of the attractions today. These and the city's many green spaces (including lush Trädgårdsföreningen) contribute to the intimate small-town atmosphere of the centre, despite the major harbour and signs of industry all around. Canals wind right through the older part of town, and a popular way of sightseeing is by the broad, flat-bottomed 'paddan' boats that ply their waters. There are also boat trips round the harbour and out to Elfsborg fortress built in the 17th century to protect the harbour entrance.

Advantageous tourist tickets give unlimited travel on city transport, including the tramcars which Gothenburgers chose to retain, but you will best appreciate the narrow streets, squares and shopping precincts of the old districts on foot. Major buildings include the so-called Fish Church housing the fish and seafood market, Kronhuset (1643) with the City Museum, Kronhusbodarna whose restored boutiques and handicraft workshops create a turn-of-the-century atmosphere, and Antikhallarna (Scandinavia's largest antique market). Among several excellent collections, the Maritime Museum is dedicated to navigation, shipbuilding and fishing, and the Röhsska Museum to arts and crafts.

From the old town, broad fashionable Kungsportsavenyn, popularly known as 'Avenyn', leads to the Art Museum, Concert Hall, City Theatre and Library clustered round Carl Milles' massively muscular statue of Poseidon in Götaplatsen. Gothenburg is also famous for its sports facilities (the Scandinavium is the biggest indoor arena in Scandinavia), exhibition halls and, above all, the splendid amusement park Liseberg, its facilities for family fun, cultural entertainment, spectacular shows and gardens second only to those of Copenhagen's Tivoli.

From Gothenburg, you have easy access to the complete contrasts of the Swedish west coast: rocky Bohuslän to the north (see Lysekil) and sandy Halland to the south (see Halmstad). See also Göta Canal. *Stockholm 483km/300mi.*

Gotland   H18

(pop. 55,000) The island lies about 65km/40mi east of the mainland to which it is linked by regular air and sea services. It is about 120km/75mi long by 56km/35mi wide and is packed with interest: Bronze Age stone heaps or great ship-shaped stone burial settings, Iron Age fortresses, some of the best extant runic, or picture, stones and, above all, churches, fortifications and houses from medieval times.

Gotland reached the height of its prosperity and fame in the 13th and 14th centuries when, for a while, **Visby** (pop. 20,000) – its capital on the west coast – was one of the most powerful cities in the Hanseatic League. Subsequently it alternated between Danish and Swedish domination, finally becoming Swedish in 1645. Impressive remains survive of Visby's medieval walls, originally about 3km/2mi long and punctuated by 44 towers. The

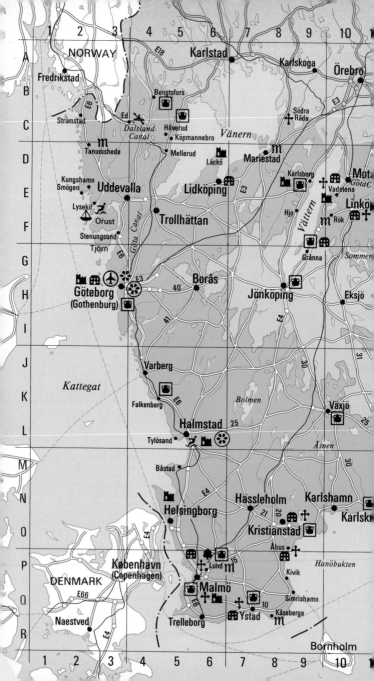

Bunge

Stord Karlsö

oldest section is the sea wall and Powder Tower, and the best view is from the north or north east. This delightful town, famous for its roses, is peppered with medieval churches, many of interest though all in ruins except for the cathedral (Sta Maria). The dramatic ruins of St Nicolaus are used for performances of the annual mystic pageant opera – *Petrus de Dacia* by Friedrich Mehler (early July-early August). It is a moving spectacle of very high standard, based on the life and writings of a 13th-century Dominican prior. Tall stepped-gable storehouses from Hanseatic times add to the medieval atmosphere; Gamla Apotek and other buildings along Strandgatan are also fine examples. The former Hanseatic harbour (Almedalen) is now a park. Gotland's Historical Museum (Fornsalen) is among the finest in Sweden (outstanding picture stones).

The island's jagged coastline is mainly steep and noted for its marine stacks, though there are excellent sandy beaches, for example, at **Tofta**, south of Visby, and **Sudersand** on Fårö. The interior consists largely of a rugged limestone plateau (*alvar*), reaching to 78m/255ft at **Lojsta**, on which you may see the attractive *russ* (half-wild ponies). There are many rare plants, including 35 species of orchid. Farming (especially livestock breeding), fishing, and the cement industry are main occupations. The northern part of Gotland, including Fårö, is a restricted area

though sites of tourist interest may be visited by foreigners (check with the tourist office). Among other main sights are **Romakloster** (12th-century ruined monastery, central Gotland), the stalactite caves of **Lummelunda** (north west), the splendid open-air museum at **Bunge** (north), and the islet of **Stora Karlsö** with its fantastic bird life (boat trips from Klintehamn). There are no less than 92 medieval churches, some, such as that of **Dalhem**, displaying beautiful stained glass.

Gotland has good sports facilities as well as its own particular Gotlandic sports, best seen during Stångaspelen, a kind of Gotland Olympics (early July), at **Stånga** in the south.

Halmstad   L5

(pop. 44,500) This is the main town on the Halland coast south of Gothenburg, famous for the long sandy beaches which have made it one of Sweden's most popular holiday areas. As well as bathing, there are good facilities for all kinds of water sports, several golf courses (the best at **Tylösand**), and family attractions such as Miniland on the outskirts of Halmstad. It is also an old town with a 17th-century castle and city walls. Two smaller seaside towns north of Halmstad are **Falkenberg** and **Varberg**, both with attractive old streets and timber houses. Falkenberg, on the River Ätran, is renowned for its salmon fishing right in the town; nearby,

Kalmar Castle

Ugglarp has a well-known vintage car museum. Varberg has sea links with Grenå in Denmark.

Båstad (36km/22mi S) is a well-equipped resort known as the 'Wimbledon of Scandinavia', scene of major tennis championships for over a century. The Halland hinterland has many old country churches and prehistoric remains. *Gothenburg 145km/90mi.*

Helsingborg O5

(pop. 81,000) The town faces Helsingør in Denmark (p. 41) across the narrowest part of the Sound, and Denmark and Sweden fought hard for control of it; the last battle was in 1710. Today it is a major seaport and commercial centre, with frequent ferry links to Helsingør and a regular service to Grenå, also in Denmark. A few miles north, the royal summer residence at **Sofiero** is open to the public for one hour daily. *Gothenburg 229km/142mi.*

Jönköping H8

(pop. 78,600) One of Sweden's oldest cities, nicely situated at the southern tip of Lake Vättern, this is the home of the match industry, with a Match Museum housed in the original factory. There is also a good County Museum. Mark Twain, who spent three months here, praised the fine sunsets. **Eksjö** (50km/31mi E) is charming with some of Sweden's best-preserved houses from the 17th century. To the north on the eastern shore of Vättern, **Gränna** (39km/24mi) is a small pretty town founded by Count Per Brahe in the 17th century and known for its peppermint rock. It has an interesting museum dedicated to the Arctic explorer S.A. André, who perished after attempting to fly over the North Pole by balloon. From the ruined castle of Brahehus, a little to the north, there are superb views over the lake to the long island of **Visingsö** (20 mins by ferry) where there are also a number of churches and ruins from the time of Brahe. Island sightseeing can

be done by horse-drawn charabanc. On Vättern's western shore, **Hjo** (64km/40mi N) is a former spa with turn-of-the-century elegance, and **Karlsborg** (98km/60mi N) has a mighty 19th–20th-century fortress with military museum by the Göta Canal. *Stockholm 327km/204mi.*

Kalmar L13

(pop. 32,000) Scene of the Kalmar Union in 1397 (p.9), this historic town is also known as the 'capital' of Sweden's most famous glass-making district. The medieval castle, fortified and enlarged by Gustavus Vasa in the 16th century, is a splendid sight looking across to Öland island (p. 106) to which Kalmar is linked by Europe's longest bridge (6km/4mi). After a devastating fire in 1647, Kalmar was rebuilt a short distance from the castle and is now a busy industrial centre and port. Its Baroque cathedral (by Tessin) and Town Hall are from the late 17th century.

In the thickly forested hinterland you will find some of the world's most famous glass factories. Many of them may be visited (free) and several have exhibitions and shops. The art of glass-blowing was introduced by a Venetian glass-blower invited by Gustavus Vasa in the 1550s. The oldest glassworks (1742) in Småland is **Kosta** (64km/40mi NW); **Orrefors** (42km/26mi NW) began as an ironworks even earlier (1726) but switched to glass in 1898, and its displays of historic and modern cut and engraved crystal are simply stunning.

Småland is also known for the staggering numbers it contributed to the great emigration of land-starved country folk to North America, from the 1850s. **Klasatorpet**, a typical homestead from those times, can be visited near **Långasjö** (67km/42mi SW). The poignant story of the emigrants is the theme of Vilhelm Moberg's best-selling four-part novel *The Emigrants*. He was born near **Växjö** (pop. 40,300; 111km/69mi W), still in the glass country, where the House of Emigrants is a small but exceptionally good museum which also provides a research centre for Swedish North Americans in search of their roots. In the same building is the Småland's Museum with a fine section on the history of glass. *Stockholm 393km/ 244mi.*

Karlskrona N12

(pop. 33,400) Founded in 1680 as a base for the Swedish navy, this bustling port, incorporating 33 islands, is still the fleet's headquarters. Timber-built Amiralitetskyrkan (Admiralty Church) dates from those early days and there are picturesque old quarters. The city has a very famous Maritime Museum with a particularly fine collection of figureheads. The archipelago clustering offshore is Sweden's southernmost and there are ferries to several islands. Fine examples of rock carvings may be seen at Hästhallen and Möckleryd near **Torhamn** to the south east. *Stockholm 479km/297mi.*

Kolmården D13

To the north east of Norrköping, Kolmårdens Djurpark is one of the finest zoos in Europe, and probably the largest in area. You can travel by cable car over some of its varied topography which shelters a Safari Park in five sections, a Dolphinarium and a Swedish farm of 50 years ago in action. One of the latest additions is a beautiful Ecumenical Church. *Stockholm 133km/82mi.*

Kristianstad O8

(pop. 30,800) Built in 1614 as a stronghold against Swedish attack at a time when the province of Skåne was Danish, Kristianstad is a pleasant town on the River Helge. The ramparts were torn down in the mid 19th century, but two gates (18th and 19th centuries) and some old barracks remain. There is a fine main square and a number of interesting 17th- and 18th-century buildings, one of which houses the local history museum. Another rather special collection is the Film Museum in Sweden's oldest film studio. Trefaldighetskyrkan (Trinity Church) is from the 17th century. On the Helge river estuary (21km/13mi SE), **Åhus** lost its importance with the building of Kristianstad. This charming small town developed round the great medieval castle (Aosehus), now in ruins by the habour. In Kungstugan, one of the many half-timbered houses which cluster round 13th-century Sta Maria church, the Swedish king Charles XI took refuge from the Danes in the 1670s. Åhus is a main centre for eel fishing, and smoked eel is a

particular local delicacy. *Stockholm 546km/338mi.*

Linköping E11

(pop. 41,300) This is a most attractive town whose old district (Gamla Linköping) is a cultural reservation of 17th–18th-century houses of great charm. Here, in summer, you can see craftsmen working in wood, clay or metal, and there is a spice garden in which 200 spice and medicinal plants flourish. The cathedral is from the mid 13th century with Romanesque and Gothic features. Several notable 12th-century churches in the surroundings include Kaga Kyrka with frescoes and elegant slim tower. *Stockholm 204km/126mi.*

Lund P6

(pop. 42,100) This is one of Scandinavia's most beautiful and fascinating cities, 19km/11mi NE of Malmö. It was founded by Knud (Canute) in 1020 and became Scandinavia's religious, political, cultural and commercial centre in the Middle Ages. The cathedral (1145) is the finest Romanesque building in northern

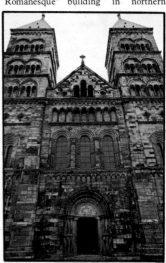

Lund Cathedral

Europe; its principal features include the 14th-century astronomic clock, 15th-century altarpiece, finely carved choir stalls and an impressive mosaic of Christ in the apse. Adjoining it is Lundagård park where the 16th-century red-brick royal residence became the university (founded 1666) and still serves as an

Rock carvings near Tanumshede

annexe to the present university (1882). There are many winding old streets such as charming Adelgatan, and in Kulturhistoriska Museet (called Kulturen) a splendid collection of old farms and manors recreates the past. The lively old-style market is held in Mårtenstorget; in a corner of the square, the stepped-gable 16th-century Krognohuset contrasts strikingly with ultramodern Lunds Konsthall art gallery. In the surrounding countryside are many traces of the past from Iron Age mounds to medieval churches, the latter including Dalby church (1060). *Gothenburg 283km/175mi.*

Lysekil   E2

(pop. 7800) This resort, about halfway between Gothenburg and the Norwegian border, is a main centre on the Bohuslän coast, a superb stretch of rocky shore and skerries whose smooth pinkish granite, much of it heather-covered, makes an aesthetic setting for bathing, sailing, windsurfing, skin diving, fishing or simply lazing. Lysekil has excellent facilities for all these activities. To the south, the labyrinthine coastal waters embrace island systems such as Orust-Tjörn, linked by soaring and dramatic road bridges to **Stenungsund** on the mainland. A string of colourful fishing communities nestle among the coves and headlands, including **Smögen** and **Kungshamn**, north of Lysekil, where you can watch the fishing fleets come and go and attend lively fish auctions. Most have small hotels or self-catering cottages.

Strömstad (pop. 4700; 95km/59mi N), close to the Norwegian border, is another attractive and lively small town clustered round its fishing and passenger harbours from which there are boat trips to **Koster islands** and to **Halden** (p. 77) in Norway. A major feature of this area are the Bronze Age rock carvings, scores of which are scattered about the countryside. The small town of **Tanumshede** is the best placed for many of them; the most important are those of nearby Vitlycke. They depict ships, animals, hunting scenes, sunworshipping and many footprints thought to be connected with some death cult. *Gothenburg 141km/87mi.*

Malmö   Q5

(pop. 235,000) Sweden's third largest city
faces Copenhagen across Öresund; the
two cities are linked by numerous ferries.
Malmö still has many lovely old buildings
from the 16th–19th centuries; Lilla Torg
is a particularly attractive square. A network of canals winds through the city and
you can travel on them by sightseeing
boat. The most interesting church is 14th-
century St Petri kyrka (St Peter's) in
Baltic Gothic style. Malmöhus Castle is a
museum complex housing art, archaeological and historical collections. Among
other museums are the Technical and
Maritime Museums and the Carriage
Museum (vehicles from the 18th century
onwards). Some of Scandinavia's oldest
monuments are to be seen in the surroundings (see Lund). *Gothenburg 290km/
180mi.*

Mariestad   D8

(pop. 17,200) This small, pretty town of
old timber houses is about halfway along
the eastern shore of Lake Vänern. The
whole countryside is dotted with prehistoric remains, rock carvings, burial
mounds and medieval churches. The
medieval church of **Södra Råda**, near
Gullspång (38km/24mi N), is particularly
notable. It has fabulous 14th-century
murals. *Stockholm 306km/190mi.*

Midsummer Festival, Öland

Öland   L14

(pop. 23,000) Though not pretty in the
conventional sense, this long thin island,
140km/87mi by 16km/10mi, is infinitely
fascinating. It is linked to Kalmar (p. 103)
on the mainland by Europe's longest
bridge (6km/4mi). Some of the most
interesting traces of Scandinavia's earliest
inhabitants are to be seen here. Bronze
and Iron Age burial mounds and grave-
fields pepper the whole island and there
are many Viking runic stones and graves.
The most spectacular gravefield is that of
Gettlinge in the south west. At the important archaeological site of **Eketorp** in
the south east, a pre-Viking ring-fort and
a later medieval settlement are under
reconstruction, using original building
methods. The main community is **Borg-
holm** (pop. 2800), a pretty little town on
the west coast, near a massive four-square
castle built by Gustavus Vasa on an earlier
foundation.

Agriculture has always been the island's
principal mainstay, though in earlier
times the farming folk were given a hard
time by raiding Danes and the greed of
Swedish kings who took the best land.
Typical features of Öland are its wind-
mills (about 400) and the communities of
enclosed farms which stand in a row
cheek-by-jowl, often with a huddle of
craftsmen's cottages nearby. The pattern
is well illustrated in the **Himmelsberga**
cultural museum (hembygdsmuseum)
near the centre of the island. Nearby at
Ismantorp are the impressive remains of
an Iron Age fort. Of several beautiful
medieval churches, one of the best preserved is at **Gärdslösa**, a little to the
north.

The southern half of the island is very
largely composed of a flat limestone plain
(*alvar*), unique in Europe. It harbours
rare plants, including many normally
found in Siberia, the Alps or eastern
Europe, among them 30 species of orchid
and 15 of violet. On the island's southern
tip, **Ottenby** bird station monitors considerable ornithological activity. The
centre of the island has extensive decidu-
ous forests, and the north has areas of
alvar and pinewoods.

Trollhättan   F4

(pop. 42,500) The town lies near the
junction of the canalized River Göta and
Lake Vänern, where the total gradient of
about 44m/144ft is negotiated by six locks,
four of them in Trollhättan. Hundreds of
thousands of visitors come annually to
watch the cargo and passenger boats passing through the lock staircase. The present locks were built in 1961, but two
earlier systems dating from 1800 and 1844
can be reached by pleasant footpaths. The
water forces, trapped by giant power
stations, are released on a few days in July
when the resulting falls attract crowds.

Castle and harbour, Vadstena

Lidköping (72km/45mi NE), on one of Vänern's southern inlets, is the home of Rörstrand, Sweden's most prestigious porcelain factory, founded in 1726; it can be visited. The town's distinctive 17th-century red Council House was originally a hunting pavilion. On a peninsula, 22km/13mi north, lakeside **Läckö Castle** is a truly impressive Baroque pile, though of much earlier origins; exhibitions are held in some of its 248 rooms in summer. *Stockholm 430km/267mi.*

Vadstena   E10

On a bay on Lake Vättern's eastern shore, this small town is a port of call on the Göta Canal route and has a number of fine old buildings, including Klosterkyrkan (the 'Blue Church'), an impressive limestone church from the early 15th century with rich interior and medieval wooden sculptures. The town is famous for its lace. The castle was founded by Gustavus Vasa in 1545. At **Rök** (30km/18mi S), the inscriptions on the largest and one of the finest runic stones (9th century) in Sweden continue to confound scholars. *Stockholm 248km/154mi.*

Ystad   R7

(pop. 14,300) This important harbour, from which there are ferry services to Rønne on the Danish island of Bornholm (p. 50), is also one of the best-preserved medieval towns in Sweden. There are about 300 half-timbered houses from the 16th century onwards, the oldest being Pilgrändsgården. Other notable buildings are Maria Church (built 13th century, enlarged in 15th), the well-preserved medieval Gråbrödrä (Grey Friars) monastery, and the Charlotte Berlins Museum, illustrating middle-class home life in the 19th century. At **Kåseberga** (19km/12mi SE), Scandinavia's largest ship-shaped stone circle (67m/220ft long) is a splendid relic of the Viking Age. A few miles east at **Backåkra**, the old farm renovated by Dag Hammarskjöld is now a museum. The sand-fringed coastline is punctuated by attractive towns such as **Simrishamn** (39km/24mi NE), Sweden's second biggest fishing port with colour-washed houses, and picturesque **Kivik** (54km/33mi NE), a fruit-growing centre where a major traditional fair is held each summer. *Stockholm 618km/384mi.*

CENTRAL SWEDEN

This region stretches from the northern sections of the great lakes of Vänern and Vättern to the borders of Sweden's far north. It includes Stockholm and its archipelago, as well as the early cultural hubs of Sweden in the surroundings, notably the former capitals of Sigtuna and Uppsala. Much of the rest is often described as 'folkloric Sweden' and folk art, music, crafts, plays, customs and traditions are all very evident. This is particularly true of the region of Dalarna (especially round Lake Siljan), with its green hills, blue lakes, red cottages, white birches and Sweden's most southerly fell district rising to 1200m/3900ft. Midsummer celebrations round decorated maypoles are particularly lively in this area. Folk art lives on in the colourfully painted wooden Dalarna horses exported all over the world, and in the costumes still worn on festive occasions and the vivid decoration of furniture and walls in the attractive old wooden houses. The people of Dalarna were god-fearing folk and the scriptures provided recurring themes in their peasant art and plays. Minerals have been mined in the region since medieval times, notably from the famous copper mine of Falun. More recently the area has spawned the great iron and steel works that are an important part of Dalarna's economy.

To the south west, the province of Värmland with its deep forests and fertile river valleys is also rich in folklore and is especially well organized for farmhouse and self-catering holidays. Hälsingland, too, bordering the Gulf of Bothnia on the main routes to the north, has several major folk gatherings.

Falun   G11
(pop. 30,100) This interesting capital of Dalarna has, since medieval times, been a major centre for copper mining. From early times it was linked by the 'Copper Way' with Røros in Norway (p. 83). Copper extraction reached its peak in the 17th century when it largely financed Sweden's part in the Thirty Years' War. After a devastating cave-in in 1687, declining production fell even further, but was later replaced by other minerals (especially iron) and chemicals, and these industries in due course expanded to other sites. Well worth visiting are the original mine and Stora Kopparbergs Museum which illustrates its history and the often grim conditions of the miners. The Dalarna Museum in Falun makes an excellent introduction to the culture of this colour-

ful province, and Kristine Church in the main square is a fine 17th-century edifice. At **Sundborn** (12km/7mi NE) the attractive home of artist Carl Larsson can be visited. *Stockholm 231km/143mi.*

Järvsö   B12
(pop. 1500) This is the best-known resort in the Ljusnan valley of Hälsingland, a region rich in folklore. Traditional skills are kept alive at the handicraft centre of Stenegården. A colourful event in July is Hälsingehambon, when about 2000 participants dance their way along the valley from **Kilafors** to Järvsö. **Delsbo**, by the wide expanses of the Dellen lakes north east of Järvsö, is another attractive centre with folk gatherings. *Stockholm 336km/208mi.*

Karlstad   L6
(pop. 51,200) This is the pleasant capital of Värmland, a province known for its literary associations (see also Sunne). Nearby **Alster** manor house, the gracious home of the great 19th-century poet Gustaf Fröding, is a museum. The town is well situated at the mouth of the River Klarälven where it flows into Lake Vänern. The Klarälven is one of Sweden's longest, mightiest rivers and annually provides a highway for millions of floating logs. At **Ransäter** (about 50km/31mi N) the childhood home of poet Eric Gustaf Geijer is another museum. The rural museum in the same village is charming and has an open-air theatre. But among the valley's most unusual attractions are the rafting holidays available on a 112km/70mi river stretch. Participants collect all their equipment at **Edebäck** (about 40km/25mi N of Ransäter) and are transported by bus to **Branäsäng** where, under supervision, they build their own rafts from 9ft logs. The gentle, idyllic journey at the river's pace of about 1mph

takes 5–7 days through wooded hills and farmland back to Edebäck. Camping equipment is provided for sleeping ashore or on the carefully moored raft. This could be the fulfilment of a dream for any would-be Huckleberry Finn. A few miles south of Edebäck the open-air museum of **Kärnåsen** is worth visiting. *Stockholm 306km/190mi.*

Örebro   L10

(pop. 88,000) The town is dominated by its 14th-century castle and the mushroom-shaped Svampen water (and view) tower, forerunner of many imitators. Above all, it makes a good launching pad for a forested lake-strewn area, excellent for such outdoor pursuits as hiking, canoeing and fishing, and dotted with communities whose origins date back to the exploitation of the rich iron ore deposits found in the Middle Ages. Of special interest is **Pershyttan**, near Nora (about 30km/18mi N), where a marked trail of 6km/4mi takes you past the old mines, furnaces, workers' houses and other paraphernalia of this ancient mining community. Another 40km/25mi NE, the village of **Grythyttan** is the attractive product of an 18th-century silver rush, with its old square, church and inn from those times. *Stockholm 196km/122mi.*

Siljan   F9

The lakes of Siljan and adjoining Orsasjön lie at the heart of a beautiful area of hills and woods, steeped in the traditions of folk culture and crafts for which Dalarna province is famous. From viewpoints such as **Åsleden** (near Leksand) reached by cable car, or **Gesundberget** (to the west of Siljan) reached by chairlift, you get a fine idea of the region. In summer regular boat services link several lakeside resorts. Here, too, the tradition of travelling to church by the distinctive long boats, reminiscent of Viking longships, is still maintained on summer Sundays, especially in **Rättvik**, and church boat races are held amid much festivity, the main event being early in July from Västanvik to Leksand.

Principal resorts are Leksand, Hjortnäs, Tällberg, Rättvik, in the south, and Mora in the north. **Leksand** (pop. 4200) is an attractive small town with a good number of old timber houses from the 16th century onwards. It was the home of Carl Hansson, the most representative of the Leksand school of painters who drew inspiration from the scriptures and the life of the people. The popular allegorical play *The Road to Heaven*, enacted in the open air at Leksand every July, is a splendid example of how God, the devil and sundry prophets and saints mingle in the affairs of

Dress from Leksand, Dalarna

Dalarna farming folk. There are many other plays of this kind in the region.

Leksand Church dates from the 13th century (rebuilt 1709–14) and has a 14th-century crucifix. A short distance north at **Hjortnäs** is the fascinating Tin Soldiers Museum, the largest of its kind in the world. A little further north, in the small resort of **Tällberg**, the attractive home of painter Gustaf Ankacrona is a museum. **Rättvik** (pop. 4000) is also the home of a painter, Målar Erik Eliasson, the first of many to create the distinctive wall paintings of floral and biblical motifs, an art form which reached its peak in the early 19th century.

On the northern shore of Siljan, **Mora** (pop. 8800) has many associations with the great artist Anders Zorn and good museums illustrating his works, as well as peasant art and architecture. Hantverksbyn is a delightful district of shops and houses recently built in traditional style. Mora is the starting point for the marathon Wasaloppet (Wasa Race) every March, when 12,000 skiers follow the route traditionally taken by Gustavus Vasa in the 16th century; it covers 85km/53mi to **Sälen** to the north west. **Våmhus** (15km/9mi N) retains the typical layout of grouped buildings where, in summer, you can watch such traditional crafts as basketwork and lacemaking from human hair. To the north, at **Fryksåsen**, an old summer farm can be seen in action in the hills above Orsasjön. **Nusnäs** (SE of Mora) is now the main source of

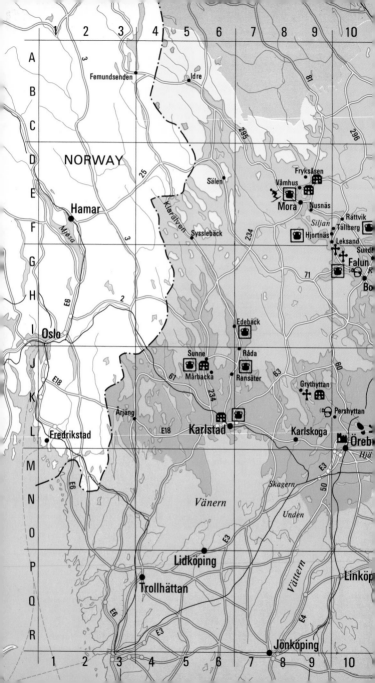

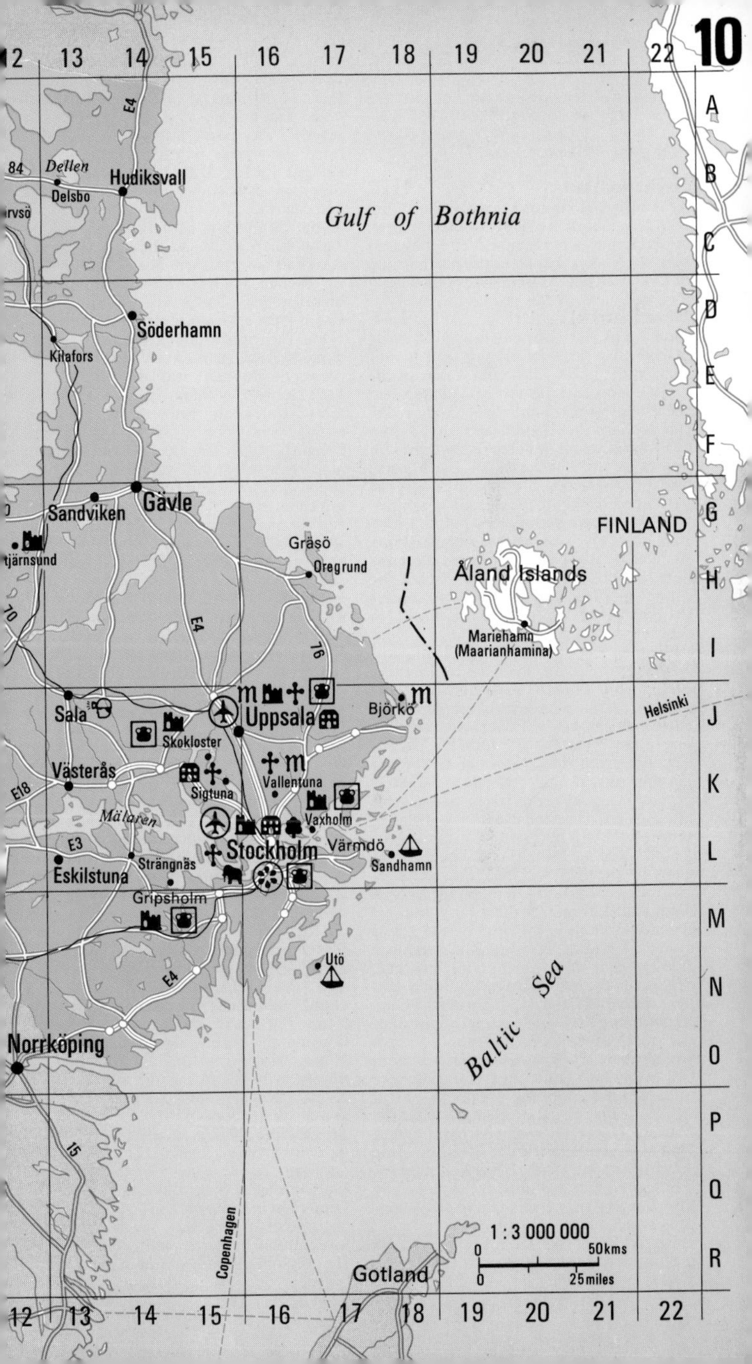

2	13	14	15	16	17	18	19	20	21	22

A
B
C
D
E
F

Dellen
Delsbo
Hudiksvall

84

rvsö

Gulf of Bothnia

Söderhamn
Kilafors

Sandviken   **Gävle**

tjärnsund

Gräsö
Oregrund

FINLAND

G

Åland Islands

H

Mariehamn
(Maarianhamina)

I

Helsinki

J

Sala

Uppsala
Skokloster

Björkö   m

Västerås

Sigtuna

Vallentuna
Vaxholm

K

Mälaren

Stockholm
Strängnäs

Värmdö

Sandhamn

L

Eskilstuna
Gripsholm

M

Norrköping

Utö

N

Baltic   Sea

O
P
Q

1 : 3 000 000

0   50 kms

R

Copenhagen

Gotland

0   25 miles

12	13	14	15	16	17	18	19	20	21	22

Dalarna wooden horses whose production dates back at least to 1840. *Rättvik–Stockholm 280km/175mi, Mora–Stockholm 319km/198mi.*

Stjärnsund   H12

This early 17th-century castle (4km/2½mi S of Askersund) is one of Sweden's finest. It perches on a peninsula above the complex waterways that form the northern tip of Lake Vättern. *Stockholm 249km/154mi.*

Stockholm   L16

(pop. 1,375,000) The city is magnificently placed on a series of islands and peninsulas at the point where the waters of the great inland lake system of Mälaren join the island-strewn Baltic Sea. Modern ferries link it to the Åland islands and Turku in Finland, and it has separate airports for domestic and international (with some domestic) services. Stockholm is best experienced by boat or on foot combined with the extremely efficient public transport network. The city was traditionally founded by Birger Jarl who built a fortress here in 1252. Gustavus Vasa made it the capital in 1523, and Gustavus Adolphus the centre of an empire in the 17th century.

Sweden House on Hamngatan makes a good starting point, for here you find the Stockholm Tourist Association information centre with the latest details of what's on and where. There are excellent one- and three-day tourist tickets, available from most newsstands, for unlimited use on city buses and underground (subway), the latter worth sampling in any case for the exotic decor of some of its stations (especially on the Blue Line). Sweden House is in the heart of the city with the main shopping and commercial area centred on Hamngatan, Sergels Torg and Hötorget. Sergels Torg, built on several levels, is dominated by the glassy modern building housing Riksdagshuset (Parliament) until 1983, while its permanent home on Helgeandsholmen islet near the Royal Palace is under restoration. Excavations there have revealed substantial traces of medieval Stockholm which will be made into a museum. Sergels Torg is a traffic hub and converging point for underground shopping precincts, one of which leads to the Central Railway Station. Hötorget, with the big Concert Hall on one side, is the site of the bustling main open-air and covered markets. These two areas are more or less linked by Drottninggatan, a lively traffic-free shopping street.

Round the corner from Sweden House is Kungsträdgården, a park where there is always plenty going on in summer from folk and pop music to top classical concerts. The outdoor chess games here and in other city parks always attract interested onlookers. South of here, several bridges lead to the Old Town (Gamla Stan) on an island. From these bridges you can watch fishermen trying their luck in the fast waters of Strömmen linking Lake Mälaren with the Baltic; you can try your luck, too, but will need a permit (ask at Sweden House). The Old Town is dominated by the massive 18th-century Royal Palace whose several museums include the beautifully arranged, award-winning Royal Armoury. The nearby cathedral (Storkyrkan) was founded in the 13th century, reconstructed in 1736; its most remarkable treasure is the great sculpture in wood of St George and the Dragon (1489). The Old Town is a maze of narrow alleys full of antique and art shops, boutiques and restaurants. Its eastern waterfront, Skeppsbron, is lined with ancient merchant buildings and, in the south, the German Church (Tyska kyrkan) has a fine mid-17th-century interior.

The Old Town is also linked to the smaller islet of Riddarholmen where most of the kings of Sweden are buried in Riddarholm Church. From its west waterfront you look across Mälaren to one of Stockholm's most distinctive buildings, the City Hall (Stadshuset) built in 1923, setting for Nobel Prize ceremonies, with its piazzalike Blue Hall and majestic Golden Hall whose walls are entirely covered with 18 million glistening mosaic tiles depicting the history of Stockholm.

Sightseeing boats leave from several points with various itineraries through the city or to the islands, one of the most popular destinations being 17th-century Drottningholm Palace set in French-style parks, housing the exquisite Court Theatre (1764–6). There are regular performances here in summer, using the original stage machinery. Regular boats also provide links with Djurgården, a chunky peninsula with very varied attractions. The boats land near the museum housing the spectacular Royal Warship *Wasa*, which capsized on her maiden voyage in 1628 and was salvaged in 1961. It has been superbly preserved and restored and is one of the top sights of Stockholm. Beside it is the pleasure garden of Gröna Lunds Tivoli, smaller and less varied than Copenhagen's or Gothenburg's, but offering plenty of family fun in summer. Beyond is Skansen, the precursor of many similar open-air museums all over the world. Here you can see over 100 buildings from many parts of Sweden, as well as demonstrations of

Drottningholm Palace

(Background) Stockholm: old town and Lake Mälaren

peasant skills. Next to it is the zoo. Two other museums in Djurgården are the Nordic Museum (showing the development of Scandinavia from the 16th century) and Prince Eugen's Waldemarsudde, his residence and art collections in lovely grounds. To the north of Djurgården is Kaknäs Tower, a fine viewpoint from the tallest building in Scandinavia (155m/508ft). Another unusual viewpoint, nearer the centre, is Katarinahissen (elevator) just south of the Old Town.

Stockholm is particularly rich in museums and has over 50 altogether: of special note are Gustavus III's Pavilion with its late 18th-century interiors, the Rosendal palace (*slott*) housing the memorabilia of the first king of the House of Bernadotte, the National Maritime Museum, and the Museum of Far Eastern Antiquities. One of the loveliest spots is north east of town at Lidingö where Millesgården, the home of the sculptor Carl Milles, is the waterside setting for his striking works, with marvellous views across to the city skyline.

Stockholm has plenty of fairly expensive night life. Many of its parks and historic buildings are used for concerts and other performances in the summer.

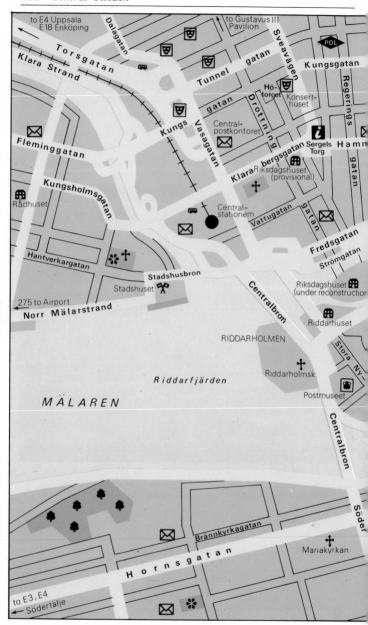

to E4 Uppsala
E18 Enköping

to Gustavus III
Pavilion

Dalagatan

Torsgatan

Klara Strand

Tunnel gatan

Sveavägen

POL

Kungsgatan

Regerings

Hö-
torget

Konsert-
huset

Kungs

Vasagatan

Drottning

Central-
postkontoret

Klara

bergsgatan

Sergels
Torg

Hamn

Fleminggatan

gatan

Riksdagshuset
(provisional)

Kungsholmsgatan

Central-
stationem

Vattugatan

gatan

Rådhuset

Fredsgatan

Hantverkargatan

Strömgatan

Stadshusbron

Centralbron

Riksdagshuset
(under reconstruction

275 to Airport

Stadshuset

Norr Mälarstrand

Riddarhuset

RIDDARHOLMEN

Stora

Ny-

Riddarfjärden

Riddarholmsk.

Postmuseet

MÄLAREN

Centralbron

Söder

Brännkyrkagatan

Hornsgatan

Mariakyrkan

to E3, E4
Södertälje

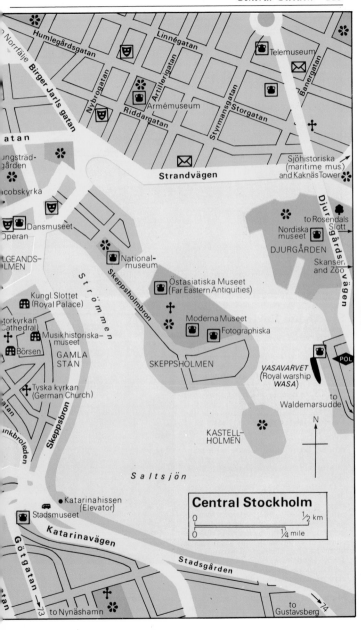

Gripsholm Castle

Stockholm Environs

Stockholm's beautiful archipelago extends for about 70km/43mi into the Baltic. The many attractive island destinations include sailing and bathing resorts, such as **Sandhamn** and **Utö**, or the townlet and museum fortress of **Vaxholm**. To the west and north are the many historic places by or near the Mälaren lake system, several of them accessible by excursion boat in summer. Westwards on the wooded island of **Björkö** are the traces of the 9th-century capital of Birka and many Viking graves. At Mariefred is 16th-century **Gripsholm Castle** with magnificent period interiors, an 18th-century theatre and Sweden's National Portrait Gallery.

Perhaps the most impressive destinations lie to the north of Stockholm. Here in the province of Uppland, about half of the 2000 runic stones in Scandinavia are to be found. A particularly interesting collection is in and beside the church of **Vallentuna**, only a short drive from the city. Lakeside **Sigtuna** (pop. 4800; 43km/26mi) succeeded Birka as capital and is Sweden's 'oldest' town – very pretty and colourful with a minute 18th-century town hall, 13th-century Mariakyrka (15th-century mural paintings) next to the medieval ruin of St Olof. A short drive away is **Skokloster**, one of

Skokloster

Sweden's most imposing castles, a majestic Baroque edifice with superb interiors, 13th-century chapel and a vintage car museum.

Lake Mälaren

Undoubtedly, however, a major destination is **Uppsala** (pop. 101,800; 68km/42mi NW) one-time royal capital, seat of the Archbishop of Sweden and site of Scandinavia's oldest university (founded 1477). The main monuments are grouped together on the slopes above the modern town. The two dominant ones are the great four-square red castle founded by Gustavus Vasa in the 1540s, and the elegant cathedral completed in 1435, where he and, traditionally, the relics of St Erik are buried; it is the largest in Scandinavia. Don't miss the older and cosier Holy Trinity Church almost next door. Various university buildings in the neighbourhood include the great library, Carolina Rediviva. Opposite the cathedral is the macabre but fascinating domed Anatomical Theatre (1662) where public postmortems were held in a steep-sided circular auditorium. Carl von Linné, better known as Linnaeus, the father of systematic botany, studied and taught in Uppsala. His town and country homes are now museums. In Old Uppsala (3km/2mi N), once the centre of heathen Sweden, you can see three great burial mounds of 6th-century Swedish kings and the flat Council Mound (Tingshögen) in a peaceful rural setting beside a 12th-century church. This was formerly a cathedral and twice its present size, but despite the ravages of fire and later additions and

changes, it is still a charming building. **Sala** (pop. 11,200; 65km/40mi W of Uppsala) is a historic silver-mining centre; one of the mines can be visited in summer.

Rottneros Manor

Sunne   J6
(pop. 4300) Three long lakes are interlinked along the very lovely Fryksdalen valley where landscapes become wilder as you travel north. Sunne is situated between two lakes and well placed for exploring the countryside so deeply associated with Sweden's most famous writer Selma Lagerlöf. Her home at **Mårbacka** is a much visited museum, and many buildings in the area are known both by their true names and by those used in her novels. One of them is beautiful lakeside Rottneros Manor (her 'Ekeby'), its grounds graced by a hundred fine sculptures. *Stockholm 367km/228mi.*

NORTH SWEDEN

From the mountainous spine of Scandinavia, scores of valleys rib the landscapes and link innumerable lakes on their way to the Gulf of Bothnia. Most of the big inland provinces of Jämtland and Lappland are made up of superb, rugged wilderness territory, much of it protected as national parks with a host of outdoor activities, especially hiking, canoeing and fishing. The region includes Sweden's highest mountain Kebnekaise (2123m/6965ft). Though many of the marked trails require no more than normal fitness and proper equipment, others go through rough, difficult terrain and should not be attempted alone. Guided walks and courses are arranged by the Swedish Touring Club (STF), address on p. 29.

Most of Sweden's 15,000 Same (Lapp) citizens live in this region (see also pp. 63, 91) and though the majority now follow more conventional occupations, about 2500 still live entirely or in part from reindeer breeding, a few following the herds for long distances from winter pastures in the lowlands to summer grazing grounds in the mountains. Since 1971, reindeer breeding has been reserved by law for the Same people. Church festivals and winter fairs are big events attended by those from widely scattered communities.

The mountains are rich in minerals and attracted prospectors as early as the 17th century. The story can be followed in the museums and old sites in or near such mining towns as Kiruna and Arjeplog. The influence of mining and other commercial developments was not always beneficial to the local people and, as in other parts of the world, the introduction of hard liquor and different moral standards made their impact. So did the missionary zeal with which some Christian reformers set about obliterating the shamanist cult of the Same people, with its idols and magic drums. A notable example was the puritanical teaching spread by the Swedish priest Lars Levi Laestadius in the 19th century; this embodied a form of worship in which congregations were worked up into a trance-like frenzy that, to onlookers, must have seemed closer at times to the pagan than the Christian. The influence of Laestadianism was also very strong in parts of neighbouring Norwegian and Finnish Lapland. However, the Christian church in the north dates from much earlier times and there are some charming examples of primitive chapels, including some from the 17th century, on lonely islands and remote fells.

Abisko   C6

This national park, with its Tourist Station, covers 29sq km/11sq mi of wild country about 200km/120mi north of the Arctic Circle. It is at the northern end of the King's Route (Kungsleden), a system (430km/266mi) of marked trails that leads south along the mountainous spine of Scandinavia to Ammarnäs, much of it through spectacular scenery. On the way it touches or gives access to several magnificent national parks – Stora Sjöfallets, Sareks, Padjelanta – and Sweden's highest peak Kebnekaise (2123m/6965ft). It can be joined from other points such as Saltoluokta Tourist Station. You should seek local advice about trails which can be attempted alone, and guided walks and courses. *Stockholm 1389km/863mi.*

Åre   M2

Together with neighbouring **Duved**, this forms a lively resort area, the largest winter sports centre in Sweden, but also geared to a wide range of summer activities. A cable car takes you to the summit of Åreskutan (1320m/4330ft). Ask about the low-priced Activity Pass which offers unlimited use of many local facilities. *Stockholm 665km/413mi.*

Arjeplog   H5

(pop. 1800) This beautiful place is on the Silver Route from **Skellefteå** on the Gulf of Bothnia into Norway. As early as the first half of the 17th century, silver ore was being mined at Nasafjäll, in the mountains 100km/62mi to the west, and the story is told in the town's Silver Museum. The 18th-century church has replaced one dating from those times. This is largely a Same community and an important Winter Market takes place in early March. The Silver Route also passes through **Arvidsjaur** (86km/53mi SE), another Same community where tents and

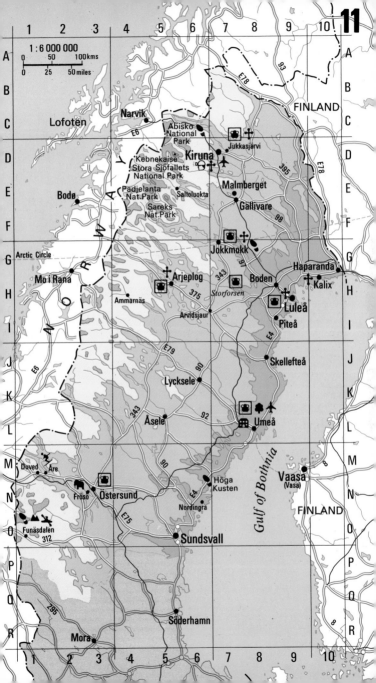

Abisko National Park

Arjeplog church

buildings from the 18th century have been preserved. Reindeer roundups are held here in June and July. *Stockholm 951km/590mi.*

Funäsdalen O1

This is the main centre for Härjedalen, one of the country's most mountainous areas. The mountain ridges which form

Reindeer roundup

Altarpiece, Jukkasjärvi church

the spine of Scandinavia pass through here, with over a score of tops above 1000m/3280ft, the highest outside Lappland being Helag (1796m/5890ft). This is wilderness country, where elk, reindeer, wolverine, marten, otter, beaver and a handful of musk ox roam. Canoes can be rented and there is plenty of excellent fishing. Marked trails are classified according to difficulty and guides can be arranged. *Stockholm 560km/347mi.*

Jokkmokk   G7

(pop. 3200) Just north of the Arctic Circle, this small town serves several major hydro-electric power stations (visits arranged in summer). It is an important Same community, holding a major Winter Fair (early February), and its Arctic Circle Museum gives an excellent idea of Same life and history. The octagonal church is a replica of its 18th-century predecessor destroyed by fire. Muddus National Park, between Jokkmokk and Gällivare, is a splendid wilderness area with marked trails. *Stockholm 1072km/666mi.*

Kiruna   D7

(pop. 25,400) Iron was first exploited in this famous mining town when the railway was extended to Narvik (p. 94) in 1902. Daily mine tours are arranged. The

church (1902) whose style is inspired by Same tents, is decorated by notable artists of that period, including Prince Eugen. At **Jukkasjärvi** (22km/13mi E) a wooden church from the 17th–18th centuries has altar paintings by Bror Hjorth depicting Laestadianism (p. 118) and Same scenes. There is a homestead museum nearby. From here even the inexperienced can enjoy the thrills of shooting the rapids down the Torne river in rented rubber boats for 60km/37mi to **Pirtilahti**. *Stockholm 1287km/800mi.*

Luleå   H9

(pop. 42,200) This is the biggest town in Swedish Lapland, founded in 1621 at Gammelstad (10km/6mi N) whose 15th-century church was later expanded and, together with its surrounding dwellings, forms the largest church town in the country – well worth a visit. In Luleå the regional Nordbotten Museum has the largest Same collections anywhere. **Piteå** (41km/25miSW) is mainly industrial but with excellent beaches. Inland, the grandiose **Storforsen** (about 45km/28mi NW) are said to be Europe's biggest untamed rapids and waterfall (81m/265ft drop). There is an interesting Forestry Museum nearby. Northwards the road leads through **Kalix** (15th-century church) to **Haparanda**

Storforsen, River Pite älv

(127km/79mi) on the Finnish border at
the outlet of the lovely Torneå valley.
From here you can make boat trips into
the Gulf of Bothnia's beautiful northernmost archipelago. *Stockholm 933km/
579mi.*

Östersund N3
(pop. 40,100) This natural gateway to the
Jämtland mountains is beautifully placed
on the intricate shoreline of Lake Storsjön
and linked by bridge to **Frösö** (good zoo)
on an island. The open-air museum of
Jämtli is interesting and there are lake
trips by old steam boat. The lake is said to
harbour a monster and in 1894 a company
was formed to catch it! All attempts failed
but the equipment used is in the County
Museum. *Stockholm 572km/355mi.*

Sundsvall O6
(pop. 55,300) This main commercial and
industrial centre on the principal coastal
highway that leads to northern Sweden
was largely rebuilt after a great fire in
1888. Regular ferries link it across the
Gulf of Bothnia with Vaasa, Finland (p.
62). It is also on the approach to the
'Steep Coast' (Höga Kusten), the most
dramatic section of Sweden's east coast,
extending north from **Sandö Bridge**
(91km/56mi N of Sundsvall) for 65km/
40mi to **Örnsköldsvik**. Here the inland

hills drop steeply to the sea, sometimes
forming sheer rocky cliffs, along a twisted
coastline of inlets and islands, its wildness
punctuated by fishing villages and red
farmsteads. The community of **Nor-
dingrå** is in the heart of the area and Höga
Kustenleden (Steep Coast Route) is a
marked hiking trail of about 40km/25mi.
Stockholm 386km/239mi.

Umeå L8
(pop. 50,000) The town is situated on the
River Umeå whose waters feed a whole
series of hydro-electric power stations and
provide a highway for millions of logs
annually. The town was rebuilt after a
great fire in 1888 and is famous for the
silver birches planted then, but typical old
buildings from the area are preserved in
the park of Gammlia, where you will also
find the County Museum. The timber-
sorting plant near the airport is an impressive sight and tours are arranged to
Stornorrfors, the giant hydro-electric
power station (15km/9mi W); a local
phenomenon is the salmon jump (*laxhop-
pet*) just below the dam. The area was the
scene of fierce fighting with the Russians
in 1809; their headquarters in an 18th-
century manor house is preserved in
Gammlia. There is a regular service across
the Gulf of Bothnia to Vaasa, Finland (p.
62). *Stockholm 661km/410mi.*

INDEX

This index is in six separate parts. The first part (below) refers to all the
general information in the book. Each of the five countries has its own index
which refers to the gazetteer. In the last five indexes all the main entries
are printed in heavy type. Map references are also printed in heavy type. The
map page number precedes the grid reference.

FINLAND

ICELAND

NORWAY

SWEDEN

128